# Tulcidious

*A Vocabulary for*

*Conscious Human Thought*

To every woman who has ever lived.

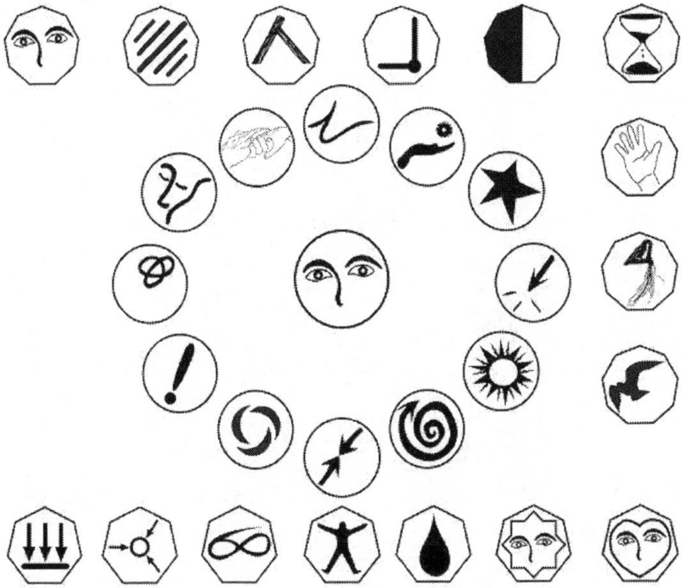

# READ THIS FIRST

It could not possibly be obvious from a first glance at twenty-nine small wooden objects that they can serve as an introductory pathway to understanding all existence. This book will offer you the possibility of seeing that pathway by identifying a three-part division among the general concepts of Creativity, Survival Skills, and the Birth of Individuality, as those ideas occur in human thinking. It is the brash and basic claim of this short book that the twenty-nine distinctions identified here in those three groups can provide a legitimate means for grasping and managing the whole of human thinking.

That such abilities might be possible to each of us may be something you have never considered. Whether you can accept these claims or not and whether or not you may hold the substantive gifts of the proposed distinctions will unfold only after you allow yourself to know the simple meaning of these twenty-nine symbolic representations. Sharing that knowledge is the first purpose of this book.

Those twenty-nine ideas and the symbolic cut-out objects at the end of this book are collectively referred to as "Tulcidious" and individually as "Tules." The first "u" in Tulcidious is pronounced like the "oo" in wool.

"Tule" is pronounced like "tool."

Tulcidious is a representational mechanism for a curriculum of thought founded in the best of human nature: the caring we each hold for our nearest and dearest. That "curriculum of thought" is a group of ideas gathered together as a vocabulary for the specific purpose of advancing the level of your own self-awareness.

This particular collection of twenty-nine ideas is also the result of a private, independent exploration into the nature and history of all existence and intelligence as best we as humans can know them both, and they constitute a vast simplification. The three questions at the heart of that exploration were "How did all this get started?" "Where does humanity stand now?" and "How can our way from here on be both aided and eased?" Tulcidious supplies a doorway to continually identifying your own most personally supportive responses to all three of these questions. The second purpose of this book is to make visible the way the Tules help to unfold meaning in our lives and how to take advantage of them.

The Tules will provide a sense of understanding and organization around the multitude of thinking events that take place for you every day. Although feelings are only occasionally mentioned specifically in the text, the Tules will also help you more fully recognize and actualize the gifts within your own feeling states. They help to ease fear and confusion in daily life.

As an explanation of the ideas represented by the individual Tules, this book is merely a beginning. You will fulfill your understanding of the Tules for yourself. In the same way that an alphabet of language provides the beginning means to make written communication possible, the Tules identify an organized and easily multi-dimensional, starting place limited only by the furthest reaches of human imagination and experience. For these reasons you may notice an intentionally brief, raw, and bare, even limited quality to what you find here. The Tules are a starting place.

The "Compendium" section is the place where the specific meaning of each individual Tule is explained. There are three distinct groups, called Full Presence (your life in creativity), The Lifeboat (essentials of survival), and The Vibrations of the Earth (the birth of individuality). Each of the three groups is explained more fully at the beginning of its section.

You will notice that the three groups of Tules can be distinguished by their shapes. The Full Presence Tules are round. There are nine

Lifeboat Tules and they are each nine-sided. There are seven Vibrations Tules and they are each seven-sided.

If you are in a rush, the introductory material at the beginning of the Compendium (page 31) and each of its three major sections are the best places to start (pages 33, 65, & 115).

You will quickly realize that the individual explanations are, for the most part, quite straightforward and simple. However, go slow. The Tules are intended to be a comprehensive source of food for thought. The text offers many examples intended to welcome both your thoughts about those examples and your reactions to the questions around how the ideas presented fit in your daily life. As you get to know them, do so as gradually as necessary to allow yourself to be guided by your own thoughts and feelings.

It is recommended that you refer to the Compendium entries in whatever order you are moved to, at first by your curiosity about the symbols. Finally, be sure to read the entire book so that you can achieve a responsible competence in your use of the Tules.

# Contents

## Introduction

Tulcidious is a representational collection of tools for life. This book is the instruction manual. Think of each Tule as a container for a group of ideas or a concept that begins with a relatively simple name, such as *Trust* or *Exploration,* and identifies a major component within your human awareness.

Each Tule is a doorway into an entirely distinct realm of thought within the idea defined by its name. They provide an intentionally broad invitation to the application of your own intuition which will grow as you expand your experience of using the Tules. You will ultimately define your own understanding of the Tules, yet there ***is*** a right way to begin. Allow yourself to be guided by what you read here in order to establish your initial sense of the Tules and their individual meanings.

The Tules are designed specifically to aid your growth by making you aware of natural processes already taking place within your awareness. They will advance the level at which you enjoy life by awakening you to the relationship between your activities and your nature and by making it possible for you to bring the two more successfully in line with each other.

Write in this book freely, as you see fit.

**The Vibrations of the Earth~ a birth of individual awareness.**

Tulcidious is divided into three distinct groups, identified by the symbols on the back of each Tule. The foundational group of seven Tules (presented last in the text) is called "The Vibrations of the Earth." Each Tule in this group shows an easily recognizable image of a tree on the back side. If you can consider our Earth to be a living "being" with a consciousness of its own (distinct in its nature and apart from our human forms of consciousness), then you will be able to appreciate the conception that the Vibrations Tules depict the ordered progression of stages in awareness which the Earth experienced as it came into existence.

**Full Presence~ states of being, a home for creativity.**

The first group, which contains thirteen Tules, is the "Full Presence" group. Each of these Tules displays on its back side the face of the Self, as you see on the title page of this book. Think of this as your own face. One of these Tules displays that face on both sides. This one, called "Full Presence," is the heart of all the Tules. The remaining twelve in the group depict individual "states of being," each of which can be considered a part of your moment-by-moment daily way of life. If you can accept that idea, then these twelve states of being can also be described as one source in human life of all our naturally creative ways.

**The Lifeboat~ elemental survival skills.**

The third group, of nine Tules, is "The Lifeboat." The back sides of these Tules show an image of a Lifeboat, empty and still at sea. The Lifeboat Tules represent the nine major skills humans have used throughout our long history in the struggle to survive the hostile elements of the planet.

It is easy to get confused living in our human lives. It is also easy to think that there is some pre-determined right way to deal with everything that you are confronted by in your life. It is true that you're likely to be commonly beset by other people, as well as a sense of domination rising from the culture you live in, telling you (directly or otherwise) the 'right way' to deal with anything you meet. The younger you are the more likely this is. But the right way to deal with your life is your own way.

It becomes understandable that you might ask: "Well then, how am I supposed to figure out what that is?" Clearing your mind of confusion will help. If you gain clarity about what's taking place in your mind, you can be more consciously in charge of it. Helping you do that is one of the major purposes of the Tules. Being more consciously in charge of what's taking place in your own mind will make it easier to relate to the other people you connect with in all aspects of your life.

*Another major purpose of the Tules is to help you grow your personal sense of inner strength and competence.*

1

# Getting Started

One way to begin is by bringing some order to your set. If you find value in your experience of these Tules, you may want to give them a place of their own in your home apart from the book. For now, just give them enough room on a table or desk so you can spread them out as described here.

The back of each Tule displays the image that identifies its group. A face for the Full

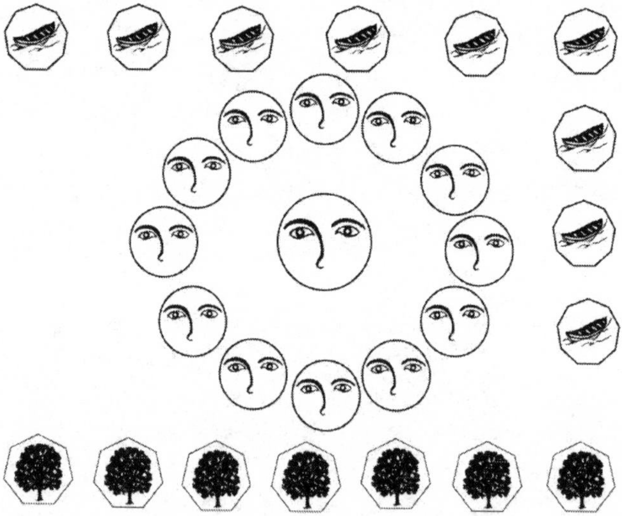

Presence group, an empty Lifeboat for that group, and a mature tree for the Vibrations of the Earth group. With these images on bottom, spread out the Tules with their faces up.

Arrange the Full Presence group in a circle, like the hours on a clock, beginning alphabetically at the one o-clock position. You may need to refer to the Compendium to match the names and symbols. Be sure to notice that the face of the Self appears in all three groups.

Spread out the Vibrations Tules below the circle to match the order shown in the layout display above, in a straight line from left to right. For the Lifeboat Tules, spread them out above the Full Presence Tules, in a line from left to right, in the order shown in the layout display above with six across the top, and the remaining three down the right side, below the sixth.

**Full Presence**

Next, begin to familiarize yourself more fully with their individual names, starting with the Full Presence group. In the layout image above, depicting their faces, the alphabetical progression begins at the one o-clock position with Blossoming, also known as Presentation. They are, in order:

Blossoming, Presentation
Declaration
Discovery
Expansion
Exploration
Focusing
Meditation
Recognition
Refinement
Rest
Thanks
Tulcidious.

Allow yourself to begin to memorize this list of names in that alphabetical order. One of the early enjoyable ways to notice the flash points in your sensate awareness is to practice identifying these twelve "states of being" by writing down their names or the symbols for each from memory, or by naming the Tules as you turn up the face of each and separating out the ones you can't name.

As you become familiar with doing that, look at what you are called to think about by the Tules whose names you were unable to remember. If, for example, you can't recall the symbol used to represent Declaration, maybe it's time to make more Declarations, or to work less at doing so, or to find out what Declarations are and start allowing yourself to understand in what way you are making Declarations at some level every moment. You are.

Keep in mind that there is no single, perfect right way to integrate this information. Memorization is suggested only as one common, familiar mechanism. The Full Presence Tules represent states of being. The Vibrations Tules represent a foundational progression of experiences. The Lifeboat Tules represent innate survival skills. The Tules themselves will help you in becoming familiar with them. Let yourself begin with the Full Presence group by memorizing those twelve names. If you are moved to do it, familiarize yourself more fully with the rest any way you like.

After you have laid the Tules out, allow yourself to think about priorities. The arrangement of the Full Presence Tules in the layout display, alphabetically and like the numbers on a clock, was set that way as an introduction. As you establish a basic understanding of their meanings, rearrange them in the way that seems the most meaningful to you now. Notice their relations. Notice which one seems most prominent to you and which one you want to think about the least. Notice what priority you might be moved to apply among them. Go slowly to respect the noticing.

The Tules are intended to serve you individually and privately. They are far more than a game. Your honesty with yourself is their lifeblood. Of course you are free to share your experience of the Tules with others, but if you find it difficult to speak honestly with others about what you see of your own life in the Tules, then be kind to yourself and refrain from making any effort to do so.

Next, turn the Tules over, mix them up completely (or close your eyes), and choose one. Admit how the idea presented by the one you chose speaks to you. Allow yourself to notice your emotional reaction to the effort you are making. If you are comfortable with them, you may begin to let the Tules contribute to your personal sense of purpose. Otherwise you will likely let them go. You may only gain a sense of their value to you as you explore and become more familiar with their individual meanings in the Compendium.

In this first intentional experience of being with the Tules, spend as much time as required to allow yourself to arrive at a completed feeling state you are willing to acknowledge, if only to yourself. When you do, that will be the end of your second meeting with the Tules. The first was when you saw them the first time. Your beginner status is now complete.

## The Vibrations of the Earth

Moving on to the Vibrations, arrange these Tules in the order shown in the second layout image. In that image, the Vibrations are the seven Tules at the bottom of the display. From left to right, they are:

Gravity, A Wave Within
Unthinkable Pressure
Multitudes Beyond Imagination
Exposure
Insanity
Trust Yourself
Love Yourself.

If you can conceive of our Earth "totalistically" as a sentient being, then you may be able to understand this order as identifying a specific progression of experience that the Earth went through in the process of coming into its conscious existence. The Vibrations Tules depict a way of understanding the Earth's birth experience. Their meanings are described individually in the Compendium.

**The Lifeboat**

Among the Lifeboat Tules (at the top and right side in the layout display) the only important specific thing is that the first one comes first. Their names, in the order shown in the layout display, beginning at the left, are:

Presence for the Self
Integrity
Trust
Responsibility
Contrast
Time
Willingness
Ability
Freedom.

The Lifeboat Tules depict humanity's long struggle for survival and the opportunity to use our experience to surmount the limits we frequently impose upon ourselves.

2

## How Does A Tule Appear?

A Tule appears when you select it. Your selection of any of the Tules is an aspect of acceptance. Acceptance is an aspect of Willingness. Willingness is to have the mind favorably disposed to doing some specific thing, not refusing. The appearance of any Tule for you, then, begins when you are favorably disposed to allowing them collectively to have a useful presence or purpose in your life. That may have occurred when you chose to buy this book, or to accept it as a gift from someone else. That may be occurring now. You are the sole judge of this, but without at least that minimal level of acceptance on your part, they are meaningless.

If you have made it beyond this small, basic matter of acceptance, then the Tules and your understanding of their meanings will aid you in expanding an awareness of your own primarily thought-based functioning. They may also help you in ordering that functioning more successfully.

As you become familiar with the Tules and what they individually mean for you, beyond the basic explanations contained in this book, you may find consistencies. Allow yourself into all that this may unfold. Your expanded familiarity may also show you patterns in your functioning. Welcome what you see in this way and allow yourself to examine your feelings about the level of utility those patterned ways of functioning may hold. Allow the patterns and consistencies you find to help you look further, both into and around the relationships in your life.

Advancing your familiarity with the Tules may also cause you to find continually expanding intricacies. If an idea presented by a particular Tule becomes "old hat" for you, but the Tule keeps appearing, it is an invitation to look for new levels of meaning. When this occurs, be sure to read the Compendium entry on that Tule again.

> *Paradox reminds us that the larger the challenge, the simpler the solution.*

# 3

## The Basics of Using the Tules

These Tules are a way of addressing the question, "are you as fully engaged as you would like in the opportunity that life offers?"

Begin now again by turning them all face down, so that the backs are showing. Mix them up. Remember that the appearance of a Tule is your selection of it. Choose one. Read the full explanation of its meaning in the Compendium. Acknowledge for yourself what that Tule causes you to think or feel. Look first at the most prominent thought or feeling that comes to mind.

If you are with other people when you do this, and you notice a reluctance to be fully open about what a Tule carries you to in awareness, then it is best to use the Tules privately. One common stance in Trust will cause many to be cautious in what they choose to share with others. The Tules are primarily intended for private use, but unless you live alone, it is likely you will want to discuss your experience of the Tules with others. When the novelty wears off, use the Tules privately.

4

# Intuition, Honesty & Choice

Using the Tules regularly offers an opportunity lesson in honesty and intuition. In the realm of thought the Tules provide a natural way of applying your attention, arguably as fully as watching television or the experience of driving, though less mechanistic or debilitating than either. Once you are satisfied that you can understand and accept the attention required to use the Tules, let yourself consider the impact of two (or, as you may wish~ more) at once. Close your eyes, mix them up, choose two, and examine their meanings in the Compendium.

Remember, it is likely that you will want to come at the Tules with one or more of the specific challenges that you normally make individual choices about. It is a common human theme to seek outside support or affirmations for our actions to a greater or lesser degree. The Tules exist to splay out before you a way of identifying, understanding, and managing the prominent themes in your own thought. If you have some particularly difficult choice to make, the Tules may compel you to admit that fact but their purpose is to make you stop and think rather than to make your choices for you.

Yet the predictable may also be

inevitable. The following example may make you smile because it helps us see how entirely fluid our human ways are, how fully we cover all the gray areas: If you were to come to the Tules with some "Yes or No" question such as, "Should I date him?" and you closed your eyes and randomly chose any two Tules (which is a perfectly acceptable way of doing that), you might come up with the Lifeboat Tule, **Trust**, and the Full Presence Tule, **Exploration**. But how would you choose between the immediate messages, "Explore Trust" and "Trust Exploration?" They could seem to be contradicting each other in the face of your question.

If you were in a rush to have some such choice made for you by an outside force, it would be easy to be satisfied with whichever of those two simple answers seemed preferable in the moment, to supply the yes or no needed (if you do see two messages, the more accurate is the first that appeared). That's the predictable though, and the opportunity is instead to allow yourself a more intimate examination of the issue, rather than looking for a fast solution. The Tules exist to help you look at your choices, rather than to make them for you.

The fast solution may be all you need or want in the moment, and you will learn to use the Tules in the way you personally prefer and feel most comfortable with, but their continual invitation is to look at any such questions with your fullest honesty, rather than quickly reaching for whatever the easy or comfortable answer may be. The only pitfall here would be the failure to make the choice for yourself. The Tules will serve more effectively to identify issues, rather than as a complex coin to flip.

In using the Tules guide yourself primarily by letting them merely suggest areas within your reality to examine.

You may quickly see that every opportunity you take to consider what the Tules offer includes the invitation to face and address the matters of how you define your own sense of intuition and how honest you are with yourself.

Remember that this process the Tules are intended to initiate in your life is a private one. The largest challenge you will find in the Tules is the choice to complete the reading of this entire book. The gifts of the Tules can become innately natural in your life when you complete this reading. The individual objects are meant to be simple reminders, like road signs, that you can easily use to return your attention to these consistent themes in your own awareness.

The varieties of possibility in thought

that are offered through the perspective of these twenty-nine marking posts are beyond any counting, and for that reason very little specific direction is given here around the matter of how you will come to use them when they are no longer new. That's an intentional invitation to finding the best way for yourself. Intuitively.

Using your intuition is living in the truth about what you feel. Honesty is in part telling the truth about what you see. What you feel begins as accessible only to you. This means that in the realm of relationships, life will likely prove easier if we allow our sense of honesty to rule when it conflicts with our intuition. When honesty and intuition meet face to face while you are alone, let honesty enthrall your intuition. This will welcome more fully the presence of your heart.

After understanding the basics of their individual meanings as explained in the Compendium, you are the sole judge of what the appearance of any Tule or combination means for you, in any given moment. Also remain clear that the given moment is what matters. The appearance of the same one or two Tules tomorrow means a different thing than it does today. Let honesty and intuition be your sole guides.

# 5

# Expanding Your Understanding and Use of the Tules

I.

The Tules are intended to depict the features of what may be called your emotional, sensate state. They represent fibers of thought and identify elements of your awareness. Natural human tendencies might cause some to wonder why only these particular twenty-nine concepts are represented as Tules. Prominent among those left out are Choice and Understanding. The reason for this might help you understand your own nature more fully. It will certainly help you understand the Tules more fully.

Choice is a methodological act. Understanding is a result. The aspects of humanness identified by the Tules are elements of thought and awareness. The Full Presence Tules identify states of being. They are not methodologies. They are not results. They are aspects of being that may be seen like common pathways within your nature.

The Lifeboat Tules depict concepts that are abstract or generic ideas generalized from particular instances. The Vibrations Tules comprise highlights in a narrative, best efforts at transliterating distinct experiences.

II.

When a particular Tule appears, you may feel little connection to the description of its meaning found in the Compendium. This is normal.

These Tules are reminders which it is best to view as invitations, merely to consider the Compendium's offerings and ask yourself what they may mean for you today.

You are the only person who can define your relationship or experience with the Tules and what they offer in your life. Their offerings change every moment and are different for every person. Also, if anyone else ever tests you on your understanding of the Tules or the Compendium's stated meanings for them, you may fairly see your tester as mis-using both you and the Tules. The Compendium is a starting place, intended to be firm, specific, defined, and certain. We all will fulfill its purpose most when we use the Tules to allow ourselves to expand, continually adding meaning, rather than limiting or constricting our understandings.

At the level of interaction, the Tules are food for continually expanding conversation connected to your specific life experiences. The only right way to use them is to begin.

III.

When you come to see yourself as "at home" with the Tules you may want to keep them spread out face up. After all, they are mainly reminders and keeping them visible is the best way to have them accessible. When you come to this place in your experience of the Tules, allow yourself to take a few minutes each day just to be with the thoughts they provoke.

Look them over, and think through the things you are dealing with in life. Whenever a Tule stands out, read the Compendium section on its meaning. There are strong and supporting ways to view, hold, and understand your natural thinking processes and the Tules are intended to help you see those.

# 6

## The Compendium

The Compendium explains the meaning of each individual Tule. It is the central-source place for gathering those meanings as well as the correct starting ways to use Tulcidious. Until you are familiar with their meanings, refer to the Compendium's definitions and explanations for clarity about each appearance. Most of these meanings follow the dictionary definitions closely. Allow yourself to become clear about the perspective offered by the Compendium.

Throughout the individual entries in the Compendium, you will find specific suggestions of issues to examine for yourself as each Tule appears. These suggestions offer a broad generic perspective. They depict the general forms of questions to ask of yourself and they apply to the way it is suggested you use all the Tules.

The Tules consistently invite you to look within, to enter the room inside your consciousness identified by the name on each Tule, and to ask of that room what gift can be found there. As you train yourself to openly face the many challenges the questions in the Compendium will ask, you may become far more honestly familiar with your own most common ways of operating. You will see far more of what you may or may not be happy with in yourself and you will gain the opportunity of a new strength from that awareness.

A conscious commitment to allowing the benefits of the Compendium's perspective in the relationships around you can help to significantly advance the effectiveness you will know in your closest relationships.

Trust in your own ability to examine these things competently and allow yourself to be guided first by your own honesty. Be guided also by your most subtle feelings and allow yourself to face all of the issues you see. Remember that you are alone in this process. No one is looking over your shoulder as you think and allow yourself in to what a simple and sensitive honesty will offer. There is no one you are required to report to.

The most appropriate contextual way to relate to the Tules is to see them merely as *reminders*. How does the appearing Tule relate to what is taking place in your life today, tomorrow, and every other day you use them? Foremost, the Tules are about the matter of how you function in relationship with all those around you in daily life. Welcome yourself to their gifts.

## Full Presence

Full Presence is the central access point offered by the Tules, and includes learning to continually and joyfully run in wholly new directions. It is your reality, the reality of the Self, represented here by a very simple human face, the one looking back at you from this page.

Full Presence is the peacefulness resulting from a personal sense of wholeness, according to your own considered yet honest definition. A person can be in any state of "disability" and still be Fully Present.

Full Presence is also the invitation and challenge to take on a particular thought as your own. That thought is the choice to believe in yourself as simultaneously residing in a coherent and harmonious way in ***all*** of the twelve states of being that make up this group of Tules:

Blossoming, Presentation
Declaration
Discovery
Expansion

Exploration
Focusing
Meditation
Recognition
Refinement
Rest
Thanks
Tulcidious.

These twelve states of being may be seen as energetic elements that source and sustain all human creativity.

Each of these states of being is described here, in alphabetical order. They are twelve aspects of a way of thinking that is with you all the time. The appearance of this Tule includes that specific reminder.

The Full Presence group of Tules depicts humanity's engine for growth. The twelve states of being that make up this group collectively define the means by which we consistently accomplish creation in human life.

Working with this group of ideas is founded upon a view of us all individually as constantly growing. This view also voices the purpose of human life: for each of us to expand our Ability and Willingness to experience and express Love.

The appearance of this Tule is typically offering an acknowledgment of your state of well-being and harmony in the midst of all that you are dealing with in life at this time. It may also be offering the suggestion that you look at the overall matters of coherence, balance, and harmony in your life. It might be suggesting that you are out of sync in some significant way.

As with all the Tules, your own honesty and intuition are the guiding forces that define the meaningful interpretation at any given appearance of this Tule.

*Order is an aspect of Full Presence.*

## Blossoming, Presentation

To Blossom is to come into one's own, to fulfill development, like a newly discovered talent, or to make an appearance, presenting the Self for all around you to see. The symbol is a theatrical stage shaped like an open human hand, offering the first visibility of its most recent gift, which is you.

Every form of demonstration is an aspect of Blossoming.

You are sharing yourself with everyone you meet and doing this in a way that brings newness to the task in every moment, a newness that is evident for you as well as for all those you meet.

Blossoming may be seen as the energetic home of joy.

This state also includes the seemingly passive activity of allowing unfoldment, becoming exposed and opened.

You gain from yourself all of the

permission you may require in order to fulfill any act of Blossoming. That grant of permission is an aspect of Blossoming.

Blossoming is most easily recognized in the cheerful playfulness of a happy child.

Blossoming, as Presentation, includes the world of first impressions, the first impacts you create in the experience of others you have newly met.

One aspect of Blossoming is being at your work in your way, the way that works best for you.

*Can you say what being at your work in the way that works best for you actually looks like? As you examine this question, begin when you wake in the morning.*

## Declaration

Declaration is represented by any form of star.

Declaration is the act of proclaiming, announcing, or evincing a personal public notification. You are making "I am..." statements that define who you are in broad, newly honest ways. You remain open to a fiber in your being that calls for such new Declarations all the time.

You know every interaction with others as an opportunity to make new Declarations of self. You listen to others in part through the question: "Who am I?" Declaration is how you continually build new responses.

Declaration may be accomplished by speaking, either out loud or silently within. Declaration makes an idea plain in part by use of certainty, in part by use of assertion. That expressed combination of certainty and assertion, when spoken aloud, is also the means by which you evince commitment in the world of relationship around you.

Declarations may also be accomplished through your actions.

Declarations are the result of choice.

Declaration, whether expressed or implicit in our actions, is the means by which we accomplish and maintain all personal relationship.

Declarations are frequently used to define personal realities and are at the essence of all human interaction.

Declaration's root and source, like that of all the Full Presence Tules, is the Sixth Vibration ~ Trust Yourself.

Loyalty may come to life as the result of Declaration and can become inherent in the nature of a relationship thanks to the strength of your Declarations. All oaths are Declarations.

Declaration is also a source of certainty in relationships. If you find that hard to accept, expanding the level at which you intentionally use Declaration might help.

*Consistency is an aspect of Declaration.*

## Discovery

Discovery is the act or process of unfolding the otherwise unknown. The symbol is an arrow identifying the location of your newest surprise.

You are open always to uncovering new aspects of awareness around the nature of being itself, both for yourself and for others.

You are a fulfilled expression of the continually active presence of intentional openness to everything that elevates the level at which you know yourself and the entire world around you.

In religious terms, Discovery includes the gifts of the Infinite Divine (    ).

Discovery in more specifically tangible realms is also included in the intended meaning of the concept~

What have you learned today?
What did you find today?
What did you unearth today?

Discovery is a major aspect of the process

of educating yourself and of supporting yourself. Discovery includes the moment by moment experience of the result.

You are in an active state of Discovery, at some level, every moment every day. That too is a component of creativity.

## Expansion

Expansion is the act or process of enlarging or giving yourself a greater scope. The easiest way to know this experience is to slowly take a large, deep breath. The symbol is a bright, unobstructed sun.

Expansion is elemental to the very nature of being. It is the central pro-active fiber in your emotional, sensate nature by means of which you consistently open and advance yourself further and more fully toward new realms for understanding human life and new things of all kinds.

This occurs both consciously and as an openness to readily include new aspects of awareness which has become an automatic part of your daily way of life. This is another form of contextually intentional growth.

As an Expanding being, you live in a determined knowing of yourself as such. Expansion is inherent in human nature.

Expansion has a measurable starting line in conscious growth by choice.

The desire for more individual comfort is not an aspect of Expansion. Comfort as an experience occurs as an aspect of Rest. The *desire for more* is an aspect of Integrity, the second of the Lifeboat Tules.

The concept "understanding," described earlier here as a result, may also be seen as an aspect of this Tule because understanding can naturally arise by allowing yourself to Expand.

> *Have you thought recently about where you might like to go in experience and what stands between you and that?*

## Exploration

To explore is to investigate, to search, to study, to analyze, to examine, to look into something. The symbol is an arrow-pointed, outward-going spiral.

Your every daily activity continually opens your awareness to a newly meaningful nature in everything around you.

Unimpeded Exploration consistently accomplishes the task in a way that is fully respectful of others, is accomplished independently, and alone.

Exploration includes an attentive watching and listening. Both experimentation and explanation are aspects of Exploration.

Exploration includes traipsing around hearkening after something particular by choice, and can be dangerous.

Thinking is an aspect of Exploration. What's the main thing on your mind today?

## Focusing

To Focus is to concentrate your attention or effort on a center of activity or attraction. The symbol is two arrows, that might be seen as your eyes or hands, identifying the location of a single something.

You are capable, conscious, and ready to look carefully, fully, honestly, and openly at all that comes across your path. You stop and examine the unfamiliar, the out-of-the-ordinary, and any other thing choice gives your attention to in all events and times.

Focusing is a careful looking at all that you perceive and experience.

Focusing includes being with your own acts: acts taken, acts contemplated, and acts planned.

For most, such "being with" one's own acts is values-based. Focusing is calling your attention to those values that are individually derived. Those personal values that motivate your actions.

Focusing advances self knowledge and awareness and thrives upon an honesty around emotions, thoughts, and human body feelings that come to life when we stop to look.

*What do you see?*

## Meditation

Meditation is allowing clarity to unfold as a function of freedom from distraction. The symbol is three slivers of Moon locating an open whole.

Meditation includes the act or process of engaging in solitary contemplation and reflection. Some Meditation forms start with freeing oneself from all specific thought. Other forms begin with offering a specific object or concept of attention.

Meditation includes a choosing to be intimately engaged with the calm silence that lives within. One aspect of the Meditative life includes the possibility of a wide-scale peace at the center of your being, whatever your outward circumstances may be.

Meditation is an activity that affords an experience of the infinity of simplicity.

You are fully comfortable with solitary contemplation, as a result of which you are capable of knowing and understanding peace in the face of any distraction. Think of yourself as having a relationship with Meditation.

Some say Meditation expands peace of mind, strengthens the body's immune system, awakens regenerative energies, slows biological aging, enlivens the nervous system, and enhances creative abilities.

*How do you understand Meditation?*

## Recognition

Recognition is symbolized by the exclamation point.

Recognition is the act of admitting about yourself that you hold a particular status. You are the voice, hands, and heart of Creation itself. You know this about yourself. Others know this about you, and you and those others all know this about each other. You experience peace through these forms of knowing.

There is an aspect of Recognition that is a readiness to see yourself as a tangibly real expression of the Source or creative force so many know as the Infinite Divine (   ).

Recognition is including as a part of your reality the admission that you are a breathing expression of the living, active creating energy of the Infinite.

Recognition identifies a great gift of being. If you accept the concept, the experience of arriving upon this aspect of Recognition may include the following progression of feeling state fibers:

Yes
Of course
surprise

Yes
resignation
anger

Yes
relief
protection

Yes
Rest.

Recognition can help you see that what matters most is every single thing you think, say, and do.

Jiddu Krishnamurti, a great sage of the 20th century, used the expression, "the process of the accumulation of experience" to refer to one part of what is called Recognition here.

Recognition includes appreciation and respect for all that you see and experience in the daily life of events and in the people around you.

The heart of all human creative ability can be found here, in Recognition.

## Refinement

Refinement is any means to improve or perfect something. The symbol is a moving yet contained and rounded triquetra, depicting continual active engagement inside the whole container that is you.

In human terms, Refinement is the two part process which begins with the wholly private task of honestly looking within at the way you carry yourself in your relationships and the world around you and how satisfied you are with what you see.

The second part of the Refinement process is to personally and privately (telling no one) make the changes in your own way of operating that are called for by what you notice through that honest examination of Self.

This is choosing to change yourself in ways that are carefully and personally identified. Your every moment includes a way of being that is like polishing a valuable, almost round stone. This is where you look for the ways to improve and strengthen yourself and then consciously but privately put them into place in your own life.

Refinement induces an intimate connection with one's human body feelings and always expands simplicity, consistently making life easier.

Refinement is best viewed as inwardly unidirectional. It can be seen as the birthplace of all individual emotion.

For example, sadness such as that rising from the loss of a Loved One is an aspect of Refinement. When we lose a close friend, life changes substantially and we are unavoidably carried into revisions of reality as we have known it until then. Sadness is a feeling state we may think we are uncontrollably pulled into. However, we can also see it as the almost-automatic adjusting to those changes in our individual reality that spirit requires. Sadness is an aspect of Refinement.

Similarly, all forms of emotional pain, including depression, are aspects of Refinement. They provide a step in awareness, sometimes the first, along the way to making changes called for by reality as we individually live it. Refinement can be the means by which we meet the horrors we know and intentionally mold the experience of them to our benefit as a creative act.

The reparative activity that frees you from worry is also an aspect of Refinement. If you feel extremely fragmented or scattered in facing some feature of your daily life, what it means is that you are in the perfectly natural process of personal change, an aspect of Refinement.

Recognizing these experiences as aspects of Refinement can make it easier for you to carry yourself to a place of calm about any such emotional matters. Your ability to simply have the name for what's taking place is the start of hefting and exercising authority over it all more competently. You can say to yourself, "*Ah, I'm not being overwhelmed by an immensity of problems I can't handle. Instead, I'm in the midst of a major change and changing myself as I see necessary along the way to meet the challenge the most fully well.*" That's Refinement. That's you.

Refinement is a common experience we all live with on a daily basis. Merely understanding the nature of what you are facing and the fact that this kind of personal examination is a typical aspect of life can help you carry yourself to a place of peace about Refinement, and make it possible to come at any moment of necessary change with new equanimity. In this way, Refinement applies to all the issues you face in daily life, more than just those that make up who you are.

*Forgiveness is an aspect of Refinement. Do you see other emotional processes you experience that you would call aspects of Refinement?*

## Rest

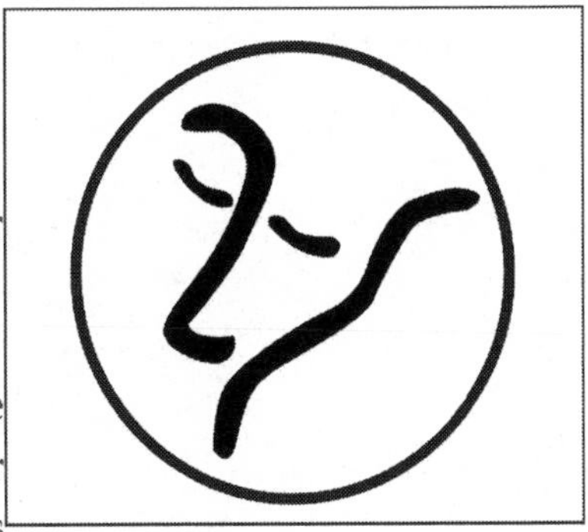

Alone in your own favorite space.

Rest is a bodily state of peace of mind or spirit. The symbol is a sleeping face.

You are expanding your readiness through relaxation at every moment, quietly and consistently advancing your sense of preparedness for all of life's frustrating confrontations.

This state includes frequent gentle calming experiences of all kinds, accomplished by choice.

Large deep breaths, which are the conscious choice to stop and breathe with awareness, bring on a state of ease, which is Rest.

Giving blood is an aspect of Rest. Simple joy can be an aspect of Rest.

Taking a walk may be Rest for you. Being alone, engaged in any form of non-stressful activity, might be Rest for you. Sleep is Rest for most. Fully engaged in some favorite activity, with the music you most like playing, might be Rest for some.

Remember that Rest, as depicted here, is an aspect of activity, or non-activity, that you are engaged in at some level every moment. You are in charge of the level at which you are Resting, always.

*Relaxation facilitates insight.*

## Thanks

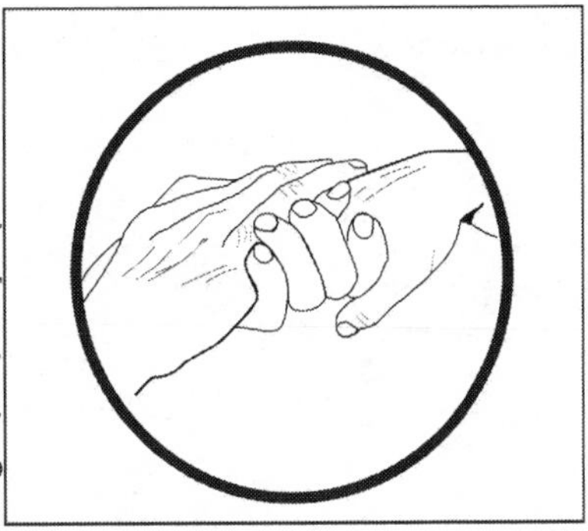

Thanks includes kindly or grateful thoughts. The symbol is one, using two hands to Thank another.

All expressions of gratitude are aspects of Thanks.

Whenever we pay anyone for anything, one of the things we are doing is expressing Thanks.

You live in appreciation. You share, experience, and think through appreciation in all that you do. This is true to the extent that you accept that idea as a component of your conscious awareness.

Thanks can have many giving forms, including congratulations, money, smiles, laughter, food, shelter, kind words spoken or written, a look in the eye, a touch of the hand, a hug, pleasure, relief, and many more.

Sharing Thanks can also be a source of joy.

## Tulcidious

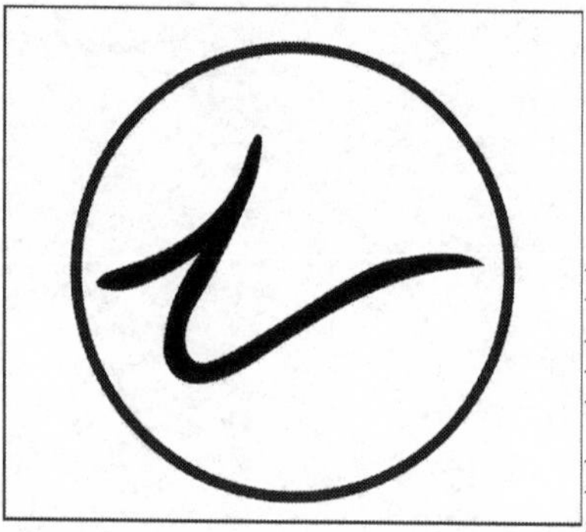

Tulcidious is living in the accomplished awareness of the wholly pervasive presence of Love in all times and places.

It is a clarity you already possess to some greater or lesser degree, in the form of an absolute, certain knowing that all is well in the accomplishment of the ultimate purposes of the universe, at that massively broad level, in your individual life, and at every level in between. Expanding your acceptance of this as an awareness can be a source of great peace.

The symbol is a single line that depicts visually a common form of the style in progression of events that advance the reality of Tulcidious in life.

See it as a bridge that picks you up gently, carries you to a great height of vision, then rather suddenly to the lowest depths, and finally very gradually allowing you out of that, leaves you again gently in a place just slightly more specifically advanced than when and where you began. Expanding moments in the conscious awareness of Tulcidious can be like that, including the greatest of highs, followed by shockingly difficult lows all of which, after complete exhaustion, can leave you in a state of gentle though great surprise, and make knowing that ultimate change very subtle, yet deeply transformative.

Advancing your awareness of the pervasive presence of Love in your life and in all human affairs is also more than a one-time experience. The Tule, Tulcidious, like all the other Full Presence Tules, identifies a state of your being, an inherent feature of your very humanness. This is true for every human.

The Tules rise from a view of reality that recognizes and respects Love as the Creative Force that carried all existence as humans can know it, all humans and all life, into being. It would serve you to glance now at your hands or into a mirror and take a moment to examine your Willingness to believe that those hands, your hands, are the hands of Love, that your face and your consciousness are a face and consciousness breathed into life by Love. You may have judgments of doubt about yourself in this regard but those are merely measures of the level of your own acceptance.

Tulcidious is an enlarged connection to all existence that expands in part by conscious choice.

Acknowledging the concept here named Tulcidious as a component or inherent "state" of your being, a connection to the accepted perfection of all human reality and all larger reality, will relieve you of fear more fully and successfully than any other act or choice you may ever know. You are certainly free to name or conceive of the experience for yourself in such terms or in any other way you like. The peculiar word, "Tulcidious" is the name the author constructed specifically as a means for acknowledging your freedom in that regard.

Tulcidious is hallmarked by the ability to recognize that every other person you come in contact with, however they may each choose to express themselves in relation to you, is expressing Love in the best way that he or she knows how, given all of that person's life, experience, and ability. Just as paying for something always includes a component of Thanks, Tulcidious reminds you that whatever else is taking place, whatever else that other person is doing, he or she, consciously or otherwise, is in part making a best effort at caring.

Tulcidious is then a multi-sensual awareness of that caring fiber in every human heart, no matter what troubles may be given life by any other being, thing, or experience. It is a "larger knowing" that transcends all contextual perceptions of conflict.

Tulcidious is the fiber in your awareness that allows you to view viciousness, and everything like it, as an aspect of either fear or confusion, or both.

Tulcidious is an invitation to consider the idea that you are inherently capable of knowing an intentional peacefulness as a defined aspect of your nature, even perhaps that such access to peacefulness is the central core of being that defines you as human.

Anger, fear, upset, conflict, and war are all aspects of Tulcidious because our ability to release these concepts from our actions and lives is accomplished by first acknowledging an identifiable reality, which is Love, known by any name we each may choose. Remember that we are all striving toward a common goal which is ultimately a mutuality. Today, in the midst of this, war isn't so much wrong as it is pointless.

Can you see it as possible for you to think that the other who is hurting you, even if in a way that you experience as intentional and malicious, is doing the best at human decency that he or she knows how (of course primarily motivated by fear) in the face of all that is his or her life? The fear that sources destructive acts most frequently rises from flawed early life training around the infinities of possibility and environments of hardship or indifference. The resultant fear is an understandable and predictable ignorance of the full nature of relationship. The ability to see and accept these ideas is also a sparking to life of compassion.

Can you see the idea that if our world exists for the purpose of expanding the genuine daily life experience of Love (kindness and caring) for us all, then confrontations with *hurt* are most accurately viewed as opportunities, something like grist for a mill that produces Love, the elemental product of all human purpose?

Can you allow yourself to see conflict as food for Love? Can you see the idea that if you are connected to some large-scale conflict like a war, your first role is to always ask, in whatever way your circumstances make possible, "why war or any form of violence at all?" Given the state of human civilization now, the same challenge applies to every smaller event of conflict in your life, far more than merely the large scale confrontations of nations and ideologies.

Even if you miss addressing this challenge, or see yourself as wholly unable to face it, merely recognizing the question is an aspect of Tulcidious and fulfills you more by advancing the pervasive presence of Love in human awareness and experience by whatever small measure your acknowledgment accomplishes. The central purpose of human existence is advanced and fulfilled more by every such acknowledgment, even if occurring only in thought. That is consciousness.

Destructive energies will always need to be stopped, but a destructive energy, unleashed by another, causes movement which can and must be dealt with, the worst effects of which may be possible to allay apart from their initiator. Separately and at the receiving end, the shift in *your* consciousness to mere awareness of our caring nature as humans can help the one who pulled the trigger to understand that doing so is pointless because this shift eviscerates the fear in you that founds the desire for revenge.

Consequences have long been a pervasive shaper of our actions. Advancing your personal sense of Tulcidious makes it possible to see a more genuine motivational reality, that unleashing destructive energies aimed at other humans is contrary to human nature. Those who continue to insist that war and any other models of problem-solving based in violence are appropriate to resolving human dilemmas, are best rightly viewed now like living dinosaurs~ ultimately extinct but undeniably large, real, and exceedingly dangerous.

Humans are all in the same predicament of frailty. This inescapable reality requires of all responsible consciousness the admission that to do harm to any other is to do harm to oneself.

Can it then be accurate to say that the crime is to be denigrated, rather than your brother, the one you would call a criminal? If you can share the strength to care for him as you do for yourself, you might come to call him by the name, Tulcidious, as a means for personally accepting our ultimately collective human mutuality.

Humanity will not fail itself because it has not committed itself to advancing to the real end of violence. If humanity fails it will be because of a denial of even the possibility that its understandable history of commitment to violence could come to a naturally evocative and fulfilling end.

How we may operate in response to such expressions as these has until now most frequently resided in a different realm, described next by the Lifeboat Tules.

## The Lifeboat

*Give a name to your choice, then ask what meaning it has in your life.*

Each of the nine Lifeboat Tules may be thought of as a multi-sided coin, even though only a single concept is specifically identified by each. In the simplest example, honesty is an aspect of Integrity (Integrity is the second Tule in the group). The phrase, "is an aspect of" is specifically intended to suggest that Integrity has many aspects, honesty being merely one of them. When the Integrity Tule appears for you, it might be an acknowledgment of (a commendation for) your honesty or it might be serving to call your attention to some ***lack*** of honesty on your part, or even on the part of others you may be dealing with. You are the judge of all such matters.

The Lifeboat Tules, in the order presented here, are:

Presence for the Self
Integrity
Trust
Responsibility
Contrast

Time
Willingness
Ability
Freedom.

Your personal honesty with yourself is the foundation on which all the Tules rest. You will succeed at using them the most effectively if you focus your attention on how they speak to or for yourself rather than the others around you.

The Lifeboat is a compilation of the primary tools humans have used for survival throughout our long history and in the process of civilizing ourselves. Their separation from the Full Presence Tules is, at the first, a way of distinguishing between the concept of survival skills and the broader realm of creativity depicted by the other group. The distinction is in part intended to show you merely one way of understanding the nature of processes you may sense in your thinking, shared with a view to making your daily life easier by helping you separate *fibers of thought* in a simple, tangible, clear and understandable way.

There is also no intent here to denigrate the concept of survival skills. They are essential basics and they hallmark major features of the successful human way. The way to most constructively use the Lifeboat Tules is to look for the opportunities of Expansion that the awareness they supply may offer.

The first is again the face of the Self. Full Presence, although here the concept is introduced with a slightly different name, which unfolds another aspect of meaning.

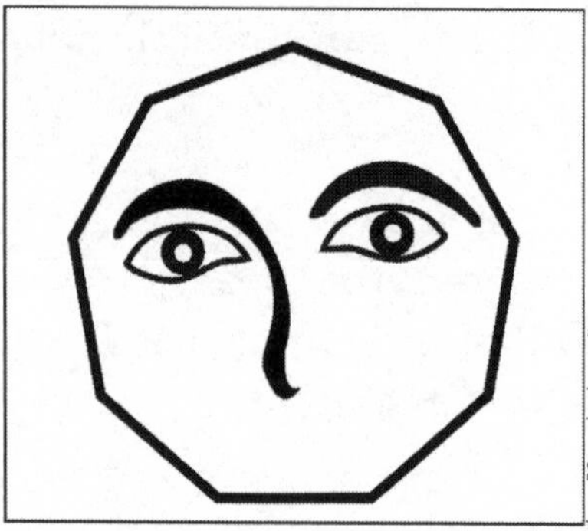

## Presence for the Self

In the movie, *Titanic,* when the last of the ship's stern finally went under, the film's hero, Jack Dawson, was pulled apart from his Love by the suction caused by the sinking ship. He was determined to make certain that Rose survived. But in order to save her, he had to first save himself from drowning. In the extreme, Presence for the Self is the choice to save yourself, as he did, in all such moments.

Being present for others necessitates being Present for the Self first. The symbol, again, is the face that represents the Self. This Tule is nine-sided, as are all the Lifeboat Tules.

Presence for the Self is an intimately connected fiber of Full Presence. As such it is rightly seen as the leading head of a tangent that proceeds out from the elemental central point of human existence and reality that your individual sense of Full Presence is. Maybe you can see the rest of the Lifeboat group of Tules as the tail of that tangent, like the tail following a comet. Imagining that tangent to be one of many may also help you to gain a perspective on the larger and more expansive features of universal reality.

In these terms, Presence for the Self is the first imperative for us all. As an imperative, it is wholly justified in all circumstances, not merely those in which our lives are threatened.

Greed, selfishness, and their more subtle forms are ***not*** aspects of Presence for the Self. Instead, they can be seen as predictable expressions occurring in relationship and, as such, aspects of Integrity, the starting place within the Lifeboat of all relationship.

Presence for the Self includes respect for yourself. The concept of mere noticing is an aspect of Presence for the Self.

Balance, in whatever form that idea has meaning for you, is an aspect of Presence for the Self.

Presence for the Self includes a conscious awareness around the elements of your individual diet. That is, everything you consume, both in terms of the food, drink, and chemical elements you send in through your mouth, nose, and skin, but also the experiences you consume on a daily basis.

If, for example, you notice that the

amount of time you spend driving a car depicts an avoidance of your intentional purposes rather than serving them, then you are missing the point, leaving yourself out, not being Present for the Self.

A chance selection of this Tule might be a commendation, or it might be a reminder to re-examine what you think is possible around the matter of how well you care for yourself. We cannot be available to serve or merely even be effectively present for others in any impactfully accomplishing way without caring for ourselves first, in all matters, times and events. This is a rule without exceptions. It may be that component in the heart of consciousness most fully affording our survival. The choice both to be and to continue to be.

And as may be gapingly plain, such an affirmation of individuality, perhaps paradoxically, fails when affirming unbridled indifference or license.

*Presence for the Self is a voice for happiness. Use it to ask yourself this question: Do you have a happy home? If you have questions about that, look at what you think is possible. One of the boundaries of reality for most is the limits defined by what we believe to be possible. Being engaged in such looking is an aspect of Presence for the Self.*

## Integrity

The ship's down. After you save yourself, do your best to help save everyone else.

This, at the very least, is kindliness, one aspect of Integrity. The symbol is a series of five individual lines depicting soundness as a whole.

Integrity is the natural state of beneficial relationship.

Integrity includes honesty, sincerity, fidelity, frankness, honor, authenticity, loyalty, respect, trustworthiness, and fairness. Integrity includes candor, which is freedom from bias, prejudice, and malice.

Although many of these features of Integrity can be listed and introduced with just one word, none of them are insignificant matters. Do you understand the meaning of each of these concepts?

Only some of the prominent features concerning Integrity are addressed here, but it is entirely appropriate to consider at a full greater length any of these listed concepts (or others you know to be features of Integrity) that attract your attention, because they all may so significantly impact the relationships in your life. In line with this reminder, be honest with yourself when facing issues that come up and examine them more carefully than you might normally.

As just one example, do you see yourself as operating *fairly* in your daily life? Fairness is characterized particularly by freedom from fraud, injustice, prejudice, and undue favoritism, even toward oneself. Looked at directly, the small four-letter word, "fair," identifies a high but appropriate standard for our Integrity. In all realms of competition, fairness includes not utilizing practices that would be condemned by law as violating the public interest. Respecting that definition, do you utilize fair practices in your daily life at work? Does your employer?

Is it also possible that your sense of Integrity would be easier to maintain if you found it meaningful to operate from a ground of being based entirely beyond competition?

Consider alternatively a ground of being based in collaboration. How does your view shift when you look for collaborative options? Does the idea of collaboration offer any meaningful or beneficial sense of purpose for you? Can you imagine that a collaborative way of being might improve your sense of personal satisfaction in the relationships around you? Can it be that widening your experience of Integrity in fairness may also rise from acknowledging a sense of connection in collaboration rather than the isolating alternative?

Integrity also includes "virtue," which is defined in part as "conformity to a standard of right" such as a sense of ethics. This is your personal connection with the standards for thought, speaking, and action that you may have chosen to respect, along with your relationship with those other persons, groups, animals, or things that are the beneficiaries of your virtue.

Your conscious choice of standards identifies the primary elemental essence of who you are. It is the founding ground in life for the possibility of the golden rule of relationship that calls us all to treat others as we ourselves wish to be treated.

The perspective offered by the Tules includes the emphatic reminder that this is a choice, calling for your fullest genuineness, rather than something pre-ordained or imposed upon you from outside. When you are aware of this choice, it will provide you great strength.

While religions, philosophies and the daily challenges of life itself may press you hard in one direction or another, you are here to give full expression to the gift of free choice that defines you, both in relationship and in how you see yourself.

The "Eightfold Path" of Buddhism can be seen as one example of a known set of standards around which you can test your personal sense of those choices you consider most meaningful. The appearance of this Tule includes the invitation to do that. Test your sense of Integrity as defined by those standards you know most precisely define you.

Deceit, greed, selfishness, and turpitude, all of which are offensive to Integrity, can in consequence be seen as aspects of it, in part because they all regard the matter of how you relate to others.

By this means, the Integrity Tule, like all the others, is specifically intended to carry your attention to concepts that could seem to be its opposites or alternatives. In simplest terms, are you operating in a manner that does harm to another? Doing any form of harm to anyone else raises the question of Integrity. Whenever you know this to be true, the question of Integrity offers the requirement of your personal and honest evaluation. To view the matter any other way is to deny another individual the level of humanity that you would grant yourself.

The Integrity Tule is also intended in part to call your attention to the reality that matters such as war and capital punishment are aspects of relationship, and hence aspects of Integrity. In today's immensely complex world, we each reach unique personal conclusions in all matters of Integrity. It is unrealistic to suggest or believe that the values we individually respect will apply with the same outcomes to all other people and circumstances. The only meaningful standard may perhaps be defined by the level of obscenity in the degree to which you believe you have a right to consciously act in a manner that produces harm or imposes suffering on others.

Remember that the Tules are not intended to define rules, but rather to reaffirm your awareness of the choices that we all face, and to call your own attention to how you resolve them. It may not be possible to define a universally consistent "right path" other than one respecting the reality that we are all unique and equally frail individuals deserving of freedom from outside oppression and entitled to each others' compassion and respect.

The Tules supply permission to expand the level at which you respect yourself. This means they are calling you to look within more fully and honestly than you ever have before at the reality of your own charge in life. They are also intended to cause you to look at issues you may never have looked directly at before, from an awareness that you are individually and exclusively the source of all of your experience.

When the Integrity Tule appears, examine the manner in which you relate to others. All of your firm "positions" in relationship are aspects of Integrity. Where you recognize your own "positionality," challenge the level of rigidity that identifies and examine whether you have formed your views for yourself. If you have not, ask yourself why.

The first time the Integrity Tule appears for you, or now, use it as an invitation to examine anew all aspects of your relational ways. Individual, familial, communal, national, human, spiritual, and metaphysical. Look at all the places you have wanted to go in relationship throughout your life until today. Look with particular care at, and question, the part that a violent state of mind may play in your thinking. Look at how you stand in your relationships. Look at what you believe to be possible in all the relationships of which you are a part. Look at the permission you grant to yourself and how this is limited by what you consider possible. Look at the degree to which your Integrity impacts all these things.

Every appearance of the Integrity Tule is an invitation into all these matters. You will experience the Tules far more successfully and with much greater strength if you will allow yourself the in-depth examination with that first appearance, or this.

Do the best you can, have fun, and be honest with yourself, knowing that you are well accompanied.

*Relationship is everything.*

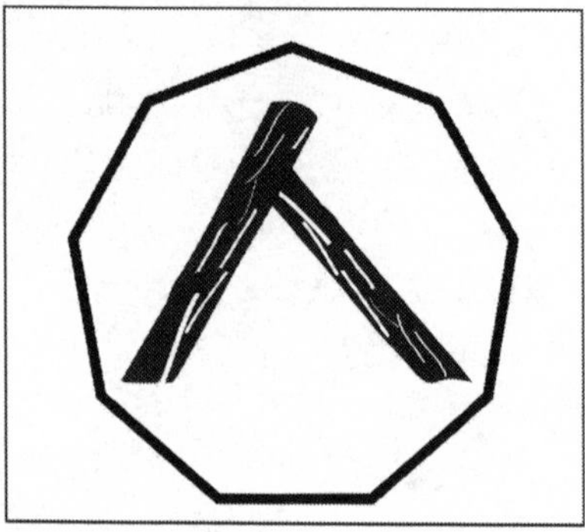

## Trust

Trust is a forward-looking, confident anticipation rising from a feeling of security and inspiring reliance upon the character, ability, strength, or truth of some other person or thing.

The symbol is one leaning on another.

This Tule concerns your Trust of others. Trust of others is one of the primary means by which we extract ourselves from the weight of individual solitude around matters of significant concern. Trust is the foundation of leadership and a primary component of constructive relationship.

When this Tule appears examine whether you can believe that opening yourself to newly Trusting another might free you from solitude around one or more of the burdens of concern you are carrying.

Sharing Trust also builds Trust (a mutuality, strengthening of everyone it touches). Expanding Trust advances the legitimacy of civilized society and can work especially well when you are confused or lost at sea and wonder why.

When you are moved or invited by the Tule to consider placing new Trust in another, remember that Trust rises from an inspiring feeling. This means that the advancement of your Trust does not rightly occur merely because you've heard that Trust is a good idea or because you read somewhere that Trust makes life easier. A hoped-for possibility of more ease is not a reason to expand your Trust. Instead, in this context the Expansion of ease is a result that can rise from a legitimately founded choice on your part. Respecting the definition of Trust stated above, this means a choice founded in your feelings, ***inspired by*** the "character, ability, strength, or truth of some other person or thing."

When this Tule appears and the opportunity to offer new Trust becomes apparent, listen to the voice of the confidence and security that your intuition may be sensing, rather than that of the fear you already know. It is inspired confidence, rather than hope for a reduction in pain or fear, that comports with the true nature of Trust.

Trust is a uniquely identifiable concept because it is forward looking and consistently involves a risk on your part that a result you may anticipate will ***not*** be fulfilled. Granting your Trust to another can be particularly risky also because it is easy to fall from a sought-after, preferred, or anticipated result to the thought that your grant of Trust permits some right to an ***expectation*** on your part, which is a form of ***requirement*** no right to which comes to life merely because you Trust someone. Mere Trust cannot guarantee a result or give you the right to require a guaranteed result. This points to one of the further realities around Trust, that you cannot precisely know in advance the exact features of the results your Trust may found.

Trust finds birth in this field of uncertainty where the risk of non-fulfillment is fully exposed. When you notice a feeling state that weakens your sense of risk, the reason may be genuine grounds for sharing your Trust.

Even if you fully understand and recognize these distinctions (and importantly if you don't), you might also feel a desire to take the risk of advancing your Trust in another without knowing this precisely identified feeling state. When you are looking to share Trust but are not moved to do so by any strong feeling of inspired ability to rely upon another, you will remain required to Trust Yourself to make the choice that accurately identifies the level of risk you are open to.

It is also true that your intuition and bodily feeling states can deliver a message so subtle, and rising from a naturalness so simple, that you may not even notice some new placement of Trust you have already accomplished. Have you begun to newly Trust someone without noticing? Have you newly noticed some long-held sense of Trust? If so, this Tule may only be aiding you in identifying a new foundation or fiber of satisfaction in your life. Perhaps new grounds for Thanks.

The Tule also invites the question whether some Trust you have already placed in another is rightly so placed. When in conscious doubt as to the rectitude of an existing placement of Trust in another person, approach that person in conversation before retreating from the tangible aspects of the investment of Trust. Communicating before withdrawing your Trust identifies commitment in your view of relationship. Reluctance in this regard identifies some experience of the opposite.

This view of Trust also identifies the importance of looking at what you use Trust to accomplish, and how you do that. This perspective on Trust may be identifying practical or responsible limits around the use of Trust. Remember that Trust, like all acts of Love, is a moment by moment outward moving cast of energy that can exist without any speaking at all. Examine carefully how you speak about Trust and what you use doing so to accomplish.

In using this and all the Tules, look for the opportunities newly offered in your life. They are invitations to that and to all the questions they inspire for you, whether stated or otherwise.

*Trust is the key to coherence.*

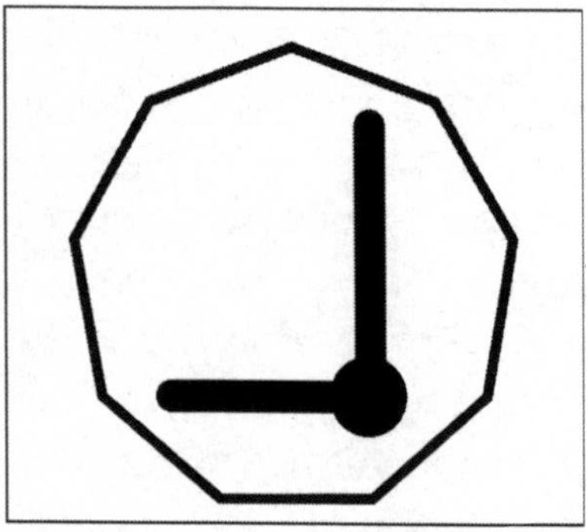

# Responsibility

Responsibility helps to provide context for our lives, most notably when we are dealing with a calamity such as a sinking ship or any other eventuality presenting the moment by moment wholly unknown. The symbol is the hands of a clock displaying the time 9 AM.

A Responsibility is an obligation in the nature of a burden which one chooses willingly to bind oneself to or accept. Such an obligation is commonly in the form of an agreement to take certain action which may or may not be specifically defined. As an example, a child's first pet would naturally come with the Responsibility for its care, although the child might not initially recognize that such Responsibility could include an array of specific activities it would become required of her to perform.

## Aspects of Responsibility~ Authority

One component of Responsibility is the authority to do the required in order to accomplish our tasks successfully. The young child's Responsibility for the care of her new puppy will then naturally include the right to tell her father when the supply of puppy food is running low. It is an important part of parenthood (and *teaching* Responsibility) to make certain that the child in such a situation is aware of this right. When we succeed at making her aware of that, then this most simple example effectively depicts the *authority* of managerial supervision. The empowered child is "in charge of" supervising the supply of dog food, an aspect of her Responsibility for the animal's care.

### Aspects of Responsibility~ Obligations

When the Responsibility Tule appears, use it first as an opportunity to look at the level at which you are succeeding with your own specifically obligated performances. Are you completely fulfilling all of what you know to be your existing Responsibilities? If you have any uncertainty in this area, the Tule is suggesting that you look very carefully to admit to yourself what you know to be the truth about that.

Because they are obligations that arise by agreement, Responsibilities are relational, involving other people. It is an irresponsible pitfall to hold undescribed expectations of other people, but it is an important part of examining one's own Responsibilities to look at what expectations others may hold of you. The expectations of others may arise as a function of the obligations you have consciously accepted as well as the stated forms of relationship you have chosen.

Paradoxically, and right or wrong, expectations concerning your obligations of action can also arise in the mind of another and begin as undescribed or unstated (not mentioned to you).

Although the unstated expectation of one does not inherently define the Responsibility of another, some Responsibilities can arise from culturally implied expectations. Other unstated Responsibilities may be imposed by law.

Responsibilities founded in culturally implied expectations are commonly seen by those others who would impose them (again rightly or wrongly) as naturally occurring and as real and firm as any fully described obligation. This reference to cultural implications acknowledges the frequently defining quality of family ties, which for many also include the influences of religious tradition. As you look at what's so for you in these areas, be both honest with and true to yourself. Culture and its attendant influences can press the most heavily into your reality when the questions at hand regard the defining of your Responsibilities, what another may believe them to be, or think or feel about how they are rightly derived.

Your mere awareness of this makes it important to face all your connections and relationships in a way that is honest and fully communicative, rather than minimal and avoiding. Doing so is a personal choice, yet the enthusiastic, honest communication being suggested can also immensely increase your strength. Be reminded again that you are the final judge of how these issues play out in your life.

You might choose one or more specific acts or courses of conduct because of the influence of some culturally oriented concept or out of a respect for an identifiable "tradition," but if you do, be certain that the choice rises from a personal conclusion about who you are rather than who someone else may wish you to be. You fail your personal identity if your choices concerning the world around you rise from anywhere other than what you know and believe of yourself from within.

The perspective from which the Tules arise includes an intent to identify a stated pathway for participation in life that would challenge you to bring yourself to the table of Responsibility with all the enthusiasm you can see to use. Have you made yourself fully aware of the obligations specifically or impliedly imposed upon you by the full array of your relationships? Have you faced your own feelings regarding the attitudes displayed by the others who may readily be willing to impose obligations upon you? At the least, these are questions about how openly you communicate. Building yourself in this area is teaching yourself with truth. Allow yourself to be ruled by who you know you are.

It can also occur that another will hold undescribed expectations of you that are not reasonable or possible to anticipate. When this occurs, it is most likely the result of that other person's fear. Remember that your choice or determination to act responsibly does not guarantee that others will do the same or even know how. How you relate to that situation is another potential entry point for both compassion and the challenge to Expand your conscious ability at communication.

In the realm of priorities, remember that the first of the Lifeboat Tules, Presence for the Self, does come first. All else yields to the imperative of your personal preservation. Unless of course the time has come to give or offer your life for something you view as having a larger or more meaningful purpose than your life in the body in which you now reside. If that is true, you would rightly be described as brave.

Responsibility defines the imperative of diplomacy.

Throughout humanity's history very many have given or risked their lives to support communal, national or religious causes they believed in, frequently considering the doing so a Responsibility. Sacrificing our lives or placing them at risk by choice in this way, however, *without a careful personal examination that respects the prior imperative of Presence for the Self and the opportunity of Integrity,* is no longer necessary and more importantly, no longer appropriate to any legitimate human purpose. Not for anyone. That "*careful personal examination that respects the prior imperative of Presence for the Self and the opportunity of Integrity,*" is the heart of Responsibility simply because, by its very nature, no Responsibility arises other than by conscious choice.

No Responsibility can be imposed upon you from outside yourself, other than by duress, which is being forced to do something against your own will. Anyone who tells you otherwise is working to deceive you, and very likely deceived themselves.

All genuine Responsibilities arise as the result of individual conscious choice. "Conscious" here means with knowledge, intent, and purpose. If you are being called upon by someone else to do something that you have not consciously chosen to accept as your obligation and if you are not moved in a current moment of newly looking to accept the obligation, then it is not your Responsibility and the most appropriate next step is to stop and ask of that other person why he or she believes otherwise.

Human history also recounts many moments like Jack Dawson's struggle for life to save the life of his Love. This may have been Jack's last intentional act. He ended his own life well used. Can it be that true Love includes the readiness to share this ultimate gift?

### Aspects of Responsibility~ Performance

Next, if there are obligations of action that you have consciously accepted and have yet to fulfill, then this Tule's appearance is a requirement that you acknowledge that fact as a way of asking yourself what is standing in the way of your performance.

When doing so, be gentle with yourself. Examining your relationship with those activities that qualify as your Responsibilities and which you have yet to fulfill advances your awareness of how you are showing up for others. When you are looking in this way, be honest with yourself and welcome your physical body feelings.

A non-performance may identify a failure of sincerity or a place of great pain. Can you see that agreeing to perform a task and leaving out the doing of it identifies a stopping place? When this is true, the Tule is intended to carry that act of stopping into your full conscious awareness, because the honest awareness puts you more fully in charge of your immediate world and reality. The Tule is inviting you to take hold of it all in an active and purposeful way.

It is a heart of honesty and a further strength to acknowledge that your status in this situation might be motivated by your own fear. If you see this situation somewhere in your life, look more deeply at what is holding you back. Fear is natural. Overcoming it is food for Love.

If you find yourself holding the strength to acknowledge a failure of sincerity on your part, which is a non-performance perhaps ***not*** rising from the feeling of having been hurt by another, you may appear indifferent. You might also be covering that indifference, even an intentional selfish indifference, with a pretense of unawareness. When this is true the motivation will likely be easier to see for those one or more others you are relating to than for you. When you can connect with one of these indicators, you will do yourself a great service to notice that you are merely facing your own fear. The bigger our fears may become the more fully they can fall, and the larger the gifts of Love they produce. Look at what will aid you in extracting yourself from this condition.

Remember that if you use your experience of this Tule to apply negative judgments to yourself for what you have yet to do, then you are misusing the opportunity and missing its gift. The Tule's purpose is the dispassionate looking that advances your conscious awareness. If you are moved to be judgmental with yourself, just stop it. Your physical-body feelings will be supplying meaningful guidance in this area.

Observing your unfulfilled Responsibilities is more tangible and real than merely conceptual. Be honest with yourself and allow the Tule's challenge that you communicate with those others to whom you may also owe that honesty.

Such an examination may also lead you to recognize that one or more of your Responsibilities are ripe for revising. Has something in relevant circumstances changed such that your consequent obligations must naturally also change? If this is true the Tule is the requirement to face the challenge to accomplish that change. Responsibilities arise in relationship and so the means by which revising them is accomplished is again a full communicative honesty, as best you are able. Is there something to say to someone in your work or personal life that you have been avoiding or newly recognize as necessary?

### Aspects of Responsibility~ New Opportunities

After you have, to your own satisfaction, honestly examined the state of your existing Responsibilities, use the appearance of this Tule to look at the question whether there are new Responsibilities offering themselves in your life. Is there an opportunity of expanded Responsibility waiting ready in your world? Is there a next larger task it is time to accept or to look for?

**Aspects of Responsibility~ Accountability**

Another element of the meaning of Responsibility is *accountability,* the readiness to be called upon to answer for your acts or choices. This is an element of maturity and depicted in far simpler terms by the following story.

The mother of two teenagers noticed that she was frustrated by a consistent habit she saw in the operating of both her children. Early on a Saturday afternoon she would ask of her daughter, "what are you and your friends doing tonight?" Her daughter would describe their plans, but consistently those plans would change any number of times across the course of the afternoon and early evening and typically end up as something never previously mentioned before her daughter actually left the house.

In some situations this can rise from a fear on the teen's part to be Responsible for making a definite choice and sticking by it. This may show a reluctance to take the risk of being judged by others (her friends) as having what might turn out to be a bad idea. It is a good example of the challenge of being that can hallmark teenage years in the United States, the challenge to take Responsibility, to say what one wants and stand by that. To be accountable, willing to be acknowledged as the cause of the result.

Again, the Tule offers the invitation to look at the places in your life now where you may rightly be facing the challenge to take new Responsibility. Look carefully, knowing that accountability comes with all new Responsibility.

**Aspects of Responsibility~ Averting Blame**

When considering the matter of Responsibility it is also easy to look to what we perceive to be the Responsibilities of others and to become judgmental. The common human tendency toward judgment is addressed in the following section describing the Contrast Tule. To be judgmental about the Responsibilities of another, however, is the dark activity of building the foundation for placing blame which is correctly addressed here, as an aspect of Responsibility.

This and all the Tules are invitations to look at the part that *you* are playing in your life, rather than anyone else's. Placing blame is an aspect of Responsibility because to place blame in another is to shirk personal Responsibility yourself or to deny holding it. So when you find yourself placing blame or whenever this Tule appears, recognize the invitation being made to both release any such judgmental thought and look instead at the opportunity offered by the circumstances to expand the measure of your own Responsibility.

When we are moved to thoughts of blame, we have already missed an opportunity of Responsibility. As suggested earlier, blame can tend to rise from the mistaken presumption of a right to require a particular result when we have shared Trust in someone else. It is important to stay aware that this discussion is about your individual emotional states around the matter of Responsibility, and not the contractual agreements we may enter into or the requirements parents may sometimes impose on children. It is a pitfall to use this view of Responsibility to examine your level of satisfaction around the performances of others. You would be serving yourself and those others far more fully by examining the quality of your own communication. To do so is to advance your own Responsibility, which is the point, to accept the stated challenge, rather than to push it off by being right about the failures of others.

The Responsibility Tule, like any other, can also appear as an acknowledgment of your successful accomplishment in any of the areas discussed here. It may be a commendation for having successfully fulfilled one or more of your existing Responsibilities or for having taken new Responsibility, having made yourself accountable in some new way that you had not thought about or had not been open to previously. As always, what's present in the moment is what counts. You alone are the judge of this. Let the Tule, whenever it appears, be a reminder of all these issues.

*A burden is an old-fashioned, unattractive name for an opportunity.*

## Contrast

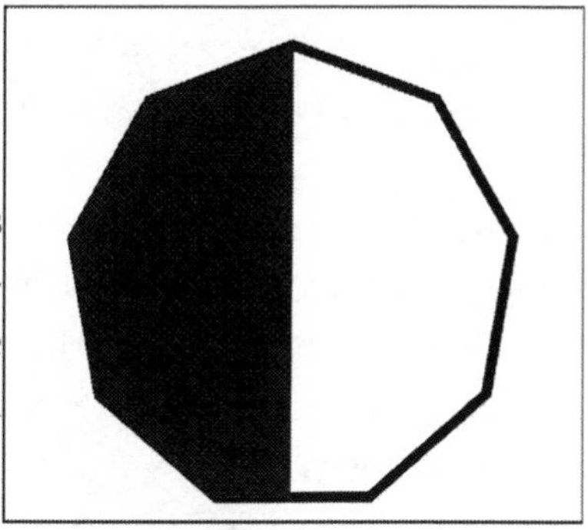

The symbol is a straight-line display of the simple difference between dark and light.

Contrast, duality, opposites. Some believe that the many dualistic pairs such as light and dark, hot and cold, right and wrong, are the primary, if not the only, means by which humans can perceive or accomplish any form of certain knowing. The purpose of this Tule is to make the strong suggestion that this is an extreme, potentially destructive, and limited view. Contrast, the examination of polarities, is merely one of many means by which reality and human activity may be understood and guided.

A major purpose of many of the most historically significant religious texts, at least as they have been used by many, is to provide guidance in understanding the basic differences between right and wrong. Systems of law can be seen in a similar way. For example, the American judicial process, by means of which all US laws are ultimately subject to being tested, accomplishes its judging purpose only when two opposing parties agree to participate by disagreeing. Is the plaintiff right and the defendant wrong or is the defendant right and the plaintiff wrong?

Some believe such tools of stark judgment are the ultimate means by which all human affairs are rightly guided. Many great books and systems have played an important role in our striving toward completion of the civilizing process in which humanity has been engaged all throughout its long history.

The judgment-process role of these books is useful but partial. Today it can be fairly suggested that they provide a limited utility, in a way that is much the same as the difference between black & white and color television. Judgment then is one of many tools by means of which human affairs can be and still are advanced.

Some consider mechanisms of judgment the ultimate. Here in the Lifeboat, however, the placement of judgment and its mechanisms, identified as aspects of Contrast, advances an important awareness by placing all such dualistic concepts and methods into a broader, totalistic perspective which is more honestly consistent with life as we know it today. From the perspective of these Tules the role of the world's religions is rightly seen in that historical context which points our attention toward relationship with what we have to revere.

While some use this opportunity to focus on conceptions around a strong sense of separated divine action as the source of human existence, from the more tangibly immediate perspective of these Tules, our most meaningfully impactful focus is our relationship with the common home that has been "mother and protector" to us all, the Earth itself.

While we can all easily differ as to the level of conscious awareness we will attribute to the Earth, our collective progress has made it possible to understand the Earth as both expanding and naturally supplying a wide variety of means for our survival. Whatever your strongest feelings in these regards may be, this Tule offers the view that all such considerations of context are aspects of Contrast.

When the Contrast Tule appears, it may mean that the time has come for you to finally resolve an important choice facing you. It might also be offering you the opportunity of examining whether the means by which you make choices reside within a relatively limited perspective.

There may be no right answer to such questions, yet facing them matters. The Tules are intended to guide you to understanding your own thought processes more fully and offering you a consistent means for opening yourself to new options within a clear and understandable framework.

If you can imagine yourself in a Lifeboat of survivors from a downed ship, the concept of Contrast is a way of offering you the warning that because you have now been thrown together with other individuals you might not have chosen in normal circumstances, it is appropriate to be prepared for the unexpected.

Many of us live large portions of our lives comfortably ensconced in a tangible and clearly understandable way that is easy for us. Striving to achieve such comfort is natural, but our comfort may leave us unaware that there are many other ways of nature and features of life the first experience of which can arrive in very stark Contrast to what we consider normal. A simple example of this is the difference between life in a western style college and life in the working world. Another is the way in which calamity and illness can suddenly and unexpectedly change our lives.

Again, the appearance of the Contrast Tule includes the warning to expect the unexpected. It offers an invitation to consider the matter of what you most like. If you see yourself as having a mature relationship with reality, the appearance of this Tule may indicate that you are somehow in the midst of the possibility of an unanticipated challenge. What do you see?

Wisdom is also an aspect of Contrast. Wisdom is typically seen as (and normally is) the advantageous product of long experience, though it also includes an authoritative quality when it comes at you from outside yourself which can be misused and lead to a perception of certainty, rigidity and domineering "rightness."

From the perspective offered by these Tules, wisdom is one of many deeply useful capacities. It is a major aspect of the purpose of this Tule to offer us all permission to carry ourselves beyond the dominance of an unexamined sense of obligation typically imposed by rigidities formed in the past.

All our lives are vastly more intricately featured now than ever before because of the rocket-speed progress of technology and the explosion of the human population. All the best voices of the past may not always hold the most appropriate definition of your next step. The appearance of this Tule is the admonition always to look for yourself.

Remember that we miss the opportunity of possibility when we think there can only be one right way. Keeping ourselves reminded that life is more than just black and white leaves us a far broader realm offering ready leaps in conscious awareness.

Every aspect of Contrast we get to know is an immensely useful mechanism for perceiving and discerning. There are many more.

*Contrast is humanity's primary hellion.*
*What classically polar or dualistic*
*controversies or conceptions do you see?*

## Time

Time is a neurological sensate mechanism through which we define and understand events. The symbol is an hourglass.

As a mechanism, Time is a tool, just as the hourglass, the sundial, and the clock are tools. This Tule invites you to acknowledge that your experience of events that are joyful is impacted significantly by the way you relate to Time. When the Time Tule appears, stop to observe your own conceptions of Time.

Some people relate to life as though there isn't enough Time, even though some major religions teach that you have an immortal (exempt from death) "soul."

Many believe we return to a new human body over and over again until all our reasons for being in human life are fulfilled. This also suggests the presence of spirit (or soul), as an aspect of your nature that is you, but somehow more all-encompassing and real than the boundaries of the body you now occupy and the limits you perceive through what you understand to be the features of human life, including Time. Some say we are spirits merely having human body experiences. Literature on what some call the "subtle body" and near-death events also depicts consciousness apart from the physical body.

If you believe your individual essence to be of spirit and if you believe further in the concept of free will, the independence to make choices for yourself, then you may be able to understand the suggestion that your presence here in human life is the result of a choice made by that larger all-encompassing essence that is your spirit. That is the choice to be in a human body, accessible to all the opportunities and subject to all the frailties which that may include, as well as all the other features of life on this planet, of which Time, as you experience it, is one.

Free will is an element of your intelligence. You've come here for a reason. Time is a tool that helps you identify your choice to be here as having a useful purpose.

If you can accept this conception of Time as a tool or skill we are somehow individually using, rather than as an element of reality we have no control over, then you may be able also to accept the suggestion that one of the prominent uses to which humans put Time is worry. If you find yourself in the Lifeboat and turn the Time Tule, look within at the level of your worry and consider the ways you can release some of it and potentially expand your joy. Frequently this shift is merely a simple choice.

Some think their available Time is a precious commodity defined by the measure of what remains between Rest periods after their Responsibilities are fulfilled. Others live to enjoy the moment by moment fulfillment of their Responsibilities, and much more. Could it be then that to choose enlivening Responsibilities is one pathway to freeing yourself from the worries that come to life within your personal conception of Time?

The appearance of this Tule is a reminder to examine anew your individual experience of Time and the impact your relationship with it has on your daily level of happiness.

If you see yourself as "trapped" by Time, running out of it or struggling with it, the appearance of this Tule is an invitation to give the matter another thought. How do you use Time? How do you find yourself handling the upsets that occur for you around Time?

Addressing these questions may make available a greater sense of control over your level of happiness than you might otherwise have imagined possible.

Time in this perspective may be viewed as the home of mathematics.

All questions have a home in Time. An example that makes this apparent is the question, "How much of your life have you devoted to what you most care about?"

If you were suddenly called upon to respond to that question, it is likely you might ask for some Time to think about it. You might also wonder why raising such a question is meaningful. These are two of the large questions that occupy the matter of knowing and clarifying who you are. Time might then also be said to be the existential home of permission.

In three words~ Now, Then, When.

*All I have Time to do is be happy.*

## Willingness

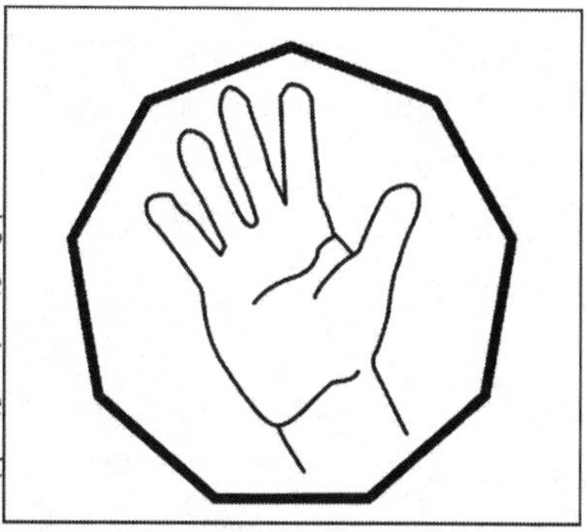

To be willing is merely to have the mind favorably disposed to doing some specified thing, not refusing.

The symbol is a raised hand indicating readiness.

Here we acknowledge the sadly obvious: nothing can constructively change in all human affairs if we lack the Willingness to allow it. Willingness is the foundation for all intentional change.

Willingness is the situation where all involved parties begin with a favorable disposition toward some identified change or resolution of a conflict. Willingness hallmarks collaborative functioning, is achievable in all circumstances, and represents one of the foundations for an ethic in human affairs that most benefits all.

Need, bravery, and self-discipline are all aspects of Willingness because they are all either motivated or resolved by it.

Refusal is an aspect of Willingness. When this Tule appears, take a look at the prominent stopping places in your life. Examine the ways you use refusal and observe what you use it to protect.

Change in human affairs is not inherently imperative, but rather consistently inevitable. This Tule offers the opportunity to examine what part you individually play in the change that has potential around you.

Do you resist the changes that offer themselves in your world? The prime focus here is not a judgment about openness to change but rather the invitation to examine the level at which your relative Willingness impacts your individual happiness and the happiness of those others in the world of relationship around you.

Willingness is the means by which fear most frequently disparages itself. Fear is one of the primary foods of Willingness. This means that your fears come to life predominantly as barriers to Willingness. When you can see this is true in particular circumstances, you can surmount your fears by consciously advancing your Willingness, however gradually as defined by your personal commitment to comfort.

Willingness, as an aspect of that which degrades fear, identifies a home and ground for bravery. In light of the measure of the impact your bravery can have, this seemingly obvious suggestion that merely toying with the idea of Willingness can be beneficial, is no small matter. Ideas have life.

The accumulation of experience, previously described as food for Recognition, is possible because of your Willingness. You might not have survived if you had failed to be Willing.

## Ability

This symbol is a sprouting seed. Ability is the potential within a seed, to open and sprout.

Ability is the skill, strength or resources necessary to perform and is found frequently as either a natural aptitude or an acquired proficiency.

You are able.

You are an individualized expression of the nature of humanity. As such, you are capable of bringing about the accomplishment of anything humans can do. Anything that you can imagine doing, you can find the way to make real. You already possess all the tools you may ever require. Any tools you may lack, you know how to obtain. The appearance of this Tule includes the invitation to examine the degree to which you believe these things.

Doubt, in the form of any lack of confidence or questioning of yourself, is an aspect of Ability. Any self-doubt is fear that places you in the Lifeboat, and has you struggling with, or at least engaged in, questions of Ability. There is nothing inherently wrong with acknowledging doubt. The Ability Tule is also intended to remind you that when in doubt, a larger perspective offers you the challenge to recognize the opportunity to grow your own sense of Ability. Doubt then, can be seen as one of the foods of Ability.

Uncertainty, which is a lack of knowledge rising around any confluence of unresolved events, is a widely common human experience and also an aspect of Ability. When you turn this Tule, look at whatever you may be dealing with that you are uncertain about. Remember that the uncertainty you may experience does not diminish your Ability. The Tule is offering you a challenge to examine what knowledge you may be lacking and how you might change that.

Ability is typically a function of what you believe to be possible. The limits you impose upon your own sense of the possible can substantially impair your Ability. Ability arises when your Willingness to make an effort exceeds the strength of those limits around possibility that you impose upon yourself.

Extenuating circumstances such as a downed ship can sometimes result in our discovering Abilities we may have long possessed but neither previously recognized nor had reason to bring to life.

> *Ability includes the fruition of imagination.*

## Freedom

Freedom is the absence of necessity, coercion or constraint in choice or action. Freedom is unimpeded access to honest truth. The symbol is a bird in flight.

Just like the concepts represented by many other Tules, Freedom is relational. The appearance of this Tule is the invitation to examine both your experience of Freedom and the ways you impact the Freedom of others.

Today, at less than the most extreme, the first Freedom is the Freedom to define Freedom for yourself, with the single proviso that in living Freedom, one may not intrude on the rights, welfare, or Freedoms of others. One aspect of Freedom then, is that respect which prevents us from doing harm to others, all while the essence of Freedom is access to honest truth.

Individual Freedom is the real foundation for all law because all law exists to protect it. Odd and basic as the idea may sound to state, Freedom includes the human Freedom merely to exist.

Any honest form of respect would, out of necessity, be a respect for all perspectives. Respecting the right to Freedom of all others will affirm your own Freedom the most fully.

Freedom is the means by which both privacy and choice are accomplished. The unimpeded right of choice is also at the heart of the nature of Freedom.

Any person who respects your right to think for yourself may fairly anticipate the ability to enjoy the same respect from you. For example, in the realm of the effort to understand ultimate questions of existence, we are each free to think for ourselves. In doing so we might each arrive, by using whatever tools we may individually have available to the purpose, at a genuine personal sense of clarity as to the nature of things, what one might call an understanding of ultimate reality. This is an aspect of the Freedom to think. Thinking about what the answers may be to ultimate questions is also an aspect of the Full Presence "state of being" known as Exploration.

One of the unfortunately repetitive practices vivid in the human way has been a concerted effort on the part of some to impose their individual or group understandings or views of ultimate realities on others. Doing so lacks respect for the reality of those others, and constitutes a theft of Freedom. In many other realms of thought humans frequently make similar efforts to impose their personally derived understandings or views on others. This lacks respect, imprisons Freedom, and denies the legitimacy of both imagination and individual intelligence which are among the elemental pillars in the advancement of human civilization. Imagination is an aspect of Freedom.

A common theme among us is to strive for truth and many succeed at deriving an individual sense of what is true. Curiously, one of the lessons of some of the most intricate works of quantum science is that the mere act of observation impacts what we see. This suggests that deriving certainty about truth may sometimes be more complicated than easy to admit.

Our striving for truth may merely be an understandable and natural striving for a sense of security. Choosing an individual understanding of the nature of truth is a right that for many resolves this striving. Many others, however, prefer to refrain from all necessity to find firm ground, gaining a sense of truth instead from a resolved absence of knowing. This is a right it is an aspect of Freedom to live.

What that means is that if you believe in

your own Freedom, you have an obligation to respect the rights of others to believe as they do and to be free from the violence that may come to life in the imposition of your view.

Your treasure might be your neighbor's garbage. Be respectful in the way you spread your treasures around.

*Your Freedom only defines mine as far as mutual respect directs us both.*

## The Vibrations of the Earth

The progression of experiences depicted by The Vibrations of the Earth supplies a firm road-bed for understanding human nature through the concept of mere being. They offer an awareness of the very coming into existence of our Earth home, not in the form of a narrative story, but as the opportunity of an experiential knowing of what is best described in human terms as a birthing.

The seven Vibrations Tules are identified here in the specific order in which the author originally experienced them~

Gravity, A Wave Within
Unthinkable Pressure
Multitudes Beyond Imagination
Exposure
Insanity
Trust Yourself
Love Yourself.

These seven Tules are the reason that the information offered in this book stands secondary to the reminders that the physical objects of the Tules themselves are. The Tules are tangible reminders to look within yourself as an entryway to interacting with and knowing your own unique and innate connection to a vastly wider consciousness that is life. The gift of this progression of experiences, identified by the Vibrations of the Earth, provided the structural context that carried into existence the remainder of the Tules and their basic division into the two distinct groups of the Lifeboat and Full Presence.

As a consequence, the Vibrations are rightly understood as the foundation for everything about how we may take in and make use of the Tules. They are depicted in the layout display at the bottom of the image to offer a visual connection to the concept of foundation.

As stated above, it is most precisely accurate to view these seven Tules as depicting the birth experience of our Earth home. Their utility in human consciousness resides in their ability to help us conceive of the immensity of the nature of force itself. A respect for the Vibrations can carry you to a real experience of boundlessness.

That sense of boundlessness and the opportunity of knowing yourself as having a grasp of limitless extent are inherent in the first five of the Vibrations. A more nearly human fiber, like a grounding in peace and strength, comes to life in the last two: Trust Yourself and Love Yourself.

Collectively, these Tules are an invitation to consider consciousness on an Earth-large scale and they offer a means for relating your individual humanity to that massive a reality.

Survival of all of the most immense extremities offered by the Earth-birthing process, at least as lived by our Earth, is yours and offers you the polite, relatively easy, but just as immense experiences of both Trusting and Loving Yourself as the fulfillment of that "process." Trusting Yourself becomes your first breath, Loving Yourself- your first meal.

Your "life" may be perceived as a reality that need never end. In individual human terms, you are full, whole, and well. You can handle anything.

## Gravity, A Wave Within

Among the first most vivid realities we all know as humans in relation to our Earth is the experience of Gravity. The symbol is three arrows pointing down to a ground that appears flat.

This is the first of the Vibrations of the Earth, the Earth's first Voice. If you will imagine being the Earth you might recognize that you would probably experience the reality of Gravity as a wave that goes inward, perhaps like an inhaling.

This experience suggests a course of coming into existence for the Earth that somehow began as a location for a gravitational reality to gather. The first humanly describable character of that experience is as an inward moving wave.

Our hearts are pumps that are in part pushing our blood in an outward direction, in waves impelled by each beat, in order to move it throughout our bodies. The Earth's own experience of Gravity is like that but of the opposite direction. It is that form of movement, that other component of our hearts' work, experienced as a wave that proceeds inward rather than outward, in human terms returning the blood to our hearts. In the realm of relational realities, that Wave Within can be seen as the first form of sensual nature for the Earth. Imagine that inward moving wave as very gentle.

Your weight is an expression of the simple constancy of that wave. That gentle inward moving wave is the Earth's heartbeat. That's Gravity, A Wave Within.

In human terms, the appearance of the Gravity Tule offers the challenge to acknowledge the undeniable features of your fundamental daily life reality, which includes the gradual unfolding of the experience that something larger is in charge and, nonetheless, you have hold. It is also an invitation to consider the possible malleability of those elements of your life that you view as the most unchangeable.

> *Your relationships with both choice and sound are aspects of Gravity.*

## Unthinkable Pressure

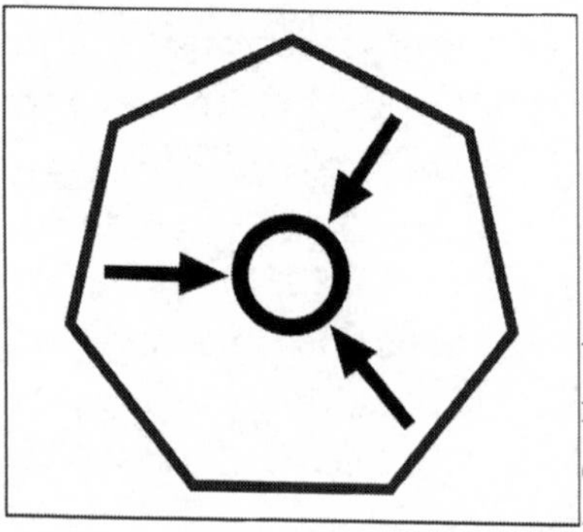

This symbol is three inward pointing arrows surrounding a circle of focus.

Distinct from Gravity, this is a multi-directional pressurizing into a great stillness. A level of pressurizing to stillness so full that it is beyond your imagination to conceive and beyond the limits of words to describe.

When the wave of Gravity accomplishes its Task of pulling inward and carries everything that is the Earth to the end of that natural path, what you are left with is the product of that unimaginable, beyond your ability to conceive, inward pressure, a pressure so full it can produce nothing more than a stillness, a stillness within which your natural and normative essence is whole and well.

Imagine now being rock. If you appreciate the utility of Meditation, go to your fullest guided-meditative state and allow yourself to imagine being rock. Then leave yourself there for as long as it takes to allow the experience through all of your chakras, all the elements of self that you know. The result can begin as frightening yet is fulfilled as a beautiful stillness because, within it all, you still breathe.

That breath is one of The Vibrations or Voices of the Earth. Its name is Unthinkable Pressure. It is Pressure beyond the measure of your ability to conceive.

An example of how this Tule can be known from the individual human perspective is a sense of absolute unshakability in resolve.

You are rock and you breathe, wholly formed, raw, new, unspecialized, complete, and well.

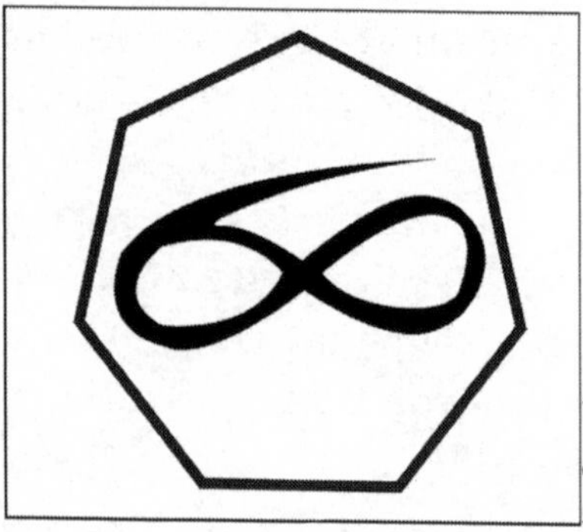

## Multitudes Beyond Imagination

This symbol is the horizontal figure-eight typically used to represent the idea of infinity, with what appears to be an escaping, arrow-pointed arc.

Multitudes Beyond Imagination is a complement to, but distinct from, Unthinkable Pressure. See them as two faces on the same coin. They are intimately similar experiences, yet described separately so that you can know them in their correct nature as distinct from each other.

Multitudes Beyond Imagination is the birth of perceptual specialization following the Unthinkable Pressure that only accomplishes the absolute maximal capable of being pressed into the reality of a single individual.

To understand Multitudes Beyond Imagination is to know yourself as one who has successfully counted all of the snowflakes that have ever fallen on the Earth throughout all time. Also, you have succeeded at counting all of our Earth's grains of sand, all of the places in space, and all of the leaves that have ever fallen and ever will.

You have fully experienced infinity in every knowable way within every realm of thought or experience where that concept has any meaning at all. You have counted everything that will meaningfully yield itself to counting. You've done it all a number of times, over and over, beyond a countable number of times.

If you have fulfilled your experience of Unthinkable Pressure, then you will be able to conceive of the arc of this symbol as not proceeding out into the unknown Multitudes, but rather delivering them to you. Here you are given a first experience of specificity, as the variety of Multitudes distinguish themselves from the mere Pressure that they might otherwise collectively comprise.

Just as Unthinkable Pressure offers a fullest experience of raw force played upon you, up to but not beyond the point of destruction, Multitudes Beyond Imagination supplies to you the means to know as part of your nature all of what that pressurizing can have arisen from, now as mere, raw possibility.

When you allow your awareness into all of that, you will know the experience as a form of strength, and the first home of vision.

Unthinkable Pressure and Multitudes Beyond Imagination are a direct pathway to unraveling an experience of the Infinite. This is one doorway to experiencing an understanding of what some scientists have referred to as the larger "Metaverse" within which the universe we know, and many others, can be said to reside or have resided.

You are invited specifically here to let your imagination run wild through the idea of counting. You are beyond counting. You know yourself as counting itself. Allow yourself into the real experience of infinity as best you can imagine it. One aspect of your human life is a wholly-inclusive transcending through containing, knowing, holding, and surmounting of all of the Multitudes of limitations that life can supply. Multitudes beyond your Imagination.

This Vibration breeds the Freedom and ability to heft and manipulate infinite possibility.

Multitudes Beyond Imagination includes a connection that makes possible knowing the use of every perceptual experience you may ever hold.

Knowing the experience Multitudes

Beyond Imagination includes the strength supplied by connection to an individual awareness of every particular desire and emotion ever known or lived by every human who ever has or ever will walk this or any other planet.

Your awareness of the concepts represented by this Tule is an element of fully knowing its complementary Tule, Unthinkable Pressure. Here you understand all of infinity-aided pressure as brought to bear upon you, within all of which, by some natural means, you have produced for yourself the ability to specify all of pressure into Multitudes so vast, beautiful, and natural that, within it all, you remain whole and well.

*You are rock and you breathe.*

## Exposure

This symbol is a stark outline of the human form, a reminder of the specific nature of your current existence, exposed.

Imagine being mere conscious existence. You are wholly round, a stone, like a marble, but with the soft skin you know now. Feel the growing, pleasureful warmth of the sun and the simultaneous coolness of a gentle breeze. A speck of sand blown by the wind touches your face and flies away. You are comfortable, at peace. Still. Alone.

Next, everything about this experience grows, ever so gradually. The sun's heat increases, eventually to the point where it burns through all the protection you can muster. The cold caused by the wind rises to meet the heat. The flying sand turns incessant, until it is wearing away at your surface. Continually and relentlessly you are being burned and frozen and blown and pelted, being worn away to something approaching nothingness.

You are eventually reduced to the

measure of a single, meaninglessly small, molecular-sized grain of sand which is finally both blown away by the wind and burned out of existence simultaneously with immense heat and cold. It is the fullest knowable devastation, but somehow your conscious essence remains. You are alive, thrive, and survive. That's Exposure.

Symbolically and maybe literally, baring your feet begins the experience of Exposure. As the question of purpose around the act of baring your feet may suggest, Exposure accomplishes a cleansing. When this Tule appears, welcome the level at which you can accept that cleansing.

As a cleansing experience, the appearance of the Exposure Tule also invites your attention to the inevitabilities within the systems of relationship of which you are a part, and suggests your examination of the feeling states that come with that.

The Exposure Tule also suggests you examine the level at which you allow yourself and your emotions to be known among those around you.

In addition, examine the impact that doing so has in defining your level of satisfaction with life as you have given it to yourself until now. Success in looking at these issues is accomplished by maintaining an observer's style of awareness while also acknowledging your presence both in and as the life observed. You are larger than all the issues and realities you face. Staying aware of this fact places those realities more fully within your control and authority.

As with all the Tules, the purpose of the examination is to support your individual sense of wholeness. When you acknowledge the seemingly hard realities you face in terms of what others may "know" about you, your attention upon this Tule serves the purpose of aiding your comfort by offering the reminder that within it all you are still more fully in charge of the circumstances than everything outside yourself.

Intelligent maturity can gain strength and peace by such means.

## Insanity

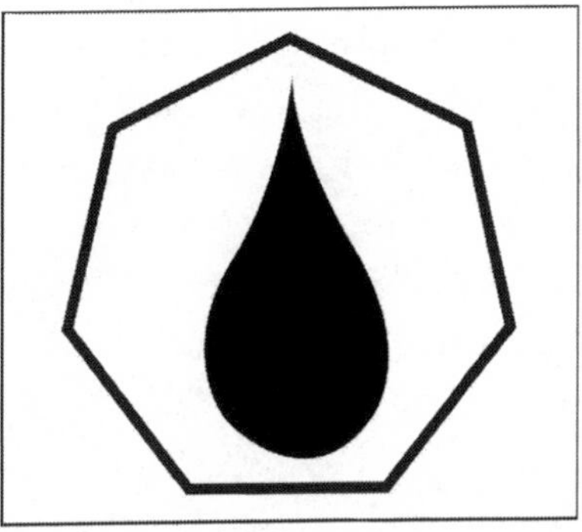

The symbol is one black tear.

You were fully exposed into nothingness (like being burned up in a fire, only more fully destroyed) and, having survived, you became completely insane. Today we know that this too is an experience you escaped and survived.

Though not before you were rendered deranged, unable to speak, unable to call for help, unable to organize thought or make sense of reality, unable to remember, unable to proceed, unable to function, unable to move, unable to plan, unable to dream, unable to rest, and unable to die.

You were petrified by the experience, stunned into helplessness and hopelessness by all external perception, sure that all accusing eyes were upon you in the fullness of the most widely and destructively negative satisfied conclusion that you were alone and personally responsible for hopeless failure. Every worst fear you ever imagined had come to pass, along with many you might never have imagined.

When this Tule appears for you, the meaningful focus is the fact that you survived, and that all of that is now mastered by you and gone. You are here with us to help us all speak more fully among ourselves about as much of it all as we can manage, for life, as fully as Love will allow.

As an example, some of humanity's survivors who have been to war prefer to refrain from speaking about their experiences. Many war veterans live with a knowing that no one else need ever be familiarized with what they have seen, lived through, known. These immense beings live like the locks on doors never to be opened because they know there is nothing to be gained by sharing what their eyes and hearts have known. For some such sharing is essential. For some it is pointless.

The result of your human connection to this awareness is a transformative strength. It is as though your skin was surgically sliced up into ribbons, doctors poked around, pushing your organs from here to there, discarding this one, adding that, then sewed you back together, the sutures held, the medications wore off, the scars affirmed, and you returned to the functional living. You are whole, yet vastly more wise, a great gift of maturity and wellness for us all.

The primary component of meaning present in the appearance of this Tule is a welcoming to move more slowly. You are a full, whole survivor, accomplished, not beset.

Be gentle with yourself. Move on.

*You are more than the worst of your own experience.*

## Trust Yourself

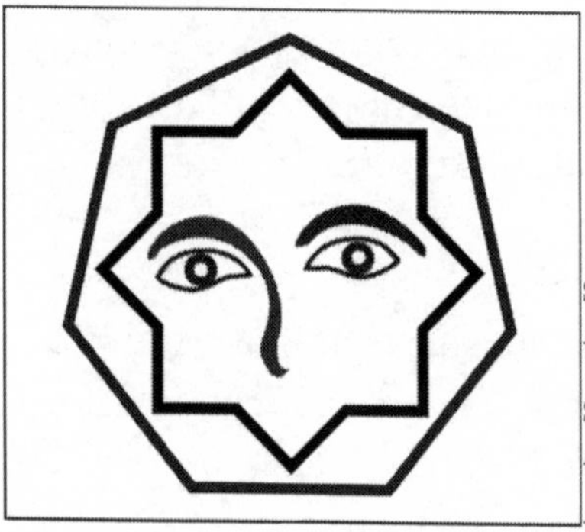

Trusting Yourself includes acceptance for Self. The symbol is the face of the Self, contained in most basic ways to affirm the formation of identity and confidence. Choosing this stance, to Trust Yourself, provides the clearest vision of all human existence throughout all of awareness and space.

After knowing the possible horror of the first five Vibrations, it is in the outset of this, the sixth, that you receive the awareness that you survived a first-consciousness experience of Gravity, a level of Pressure adequate to prove your resilience as more firm than diamond status (assuming accurately that you were already as hard as rock), that you successfully received to master multiplicitous diversity beyond all conceptions of infinity, that you were destroyed into nothingness, and lived beyond suffering any and all of the worst possible results that still surviving such an experience might mean.

You survived all of that. Congratulate yourself and begin to look around just outside your skin, recognizing that you are whole, in every way. A name for believing and living in this experience is Trust Yourself.

Trusting Yourself includes full readiness to go with your own advice when it conflicts with that of any other, even those others you already most fully Trust. The choice to do so is living that Trust.

Certainty is an aspect of Trusting Yourself. Certainty doesn't make you right or define truth. It just helps to define you as someone who Trusts Yourself.

Trusting Yourself includes believing that you are capable of making successful decisions in every aspect of your own life. It doesn't mean unrealistically thinking you know everything but it does mean understanding that you are capable and know how to get any information that may seem to be lacking when you need to make an important choice.

You know how to act in the face of lack. You know how to get what you think you need and how, who, and when to ask for help. Your feeling state will always guide you in this way. A modern novel that depicts the Sixth Vibration is Sue Monk Kidd's, *The Secret Life of Bees.*

Trusting Yourself includes allowing the

unfolding of respect for you by others and by yourself.

Trusting Yourself is the foundation and source of the Full Presence Tules which exist as a voice for all of your creative ability. In this view all of Full Presence is seen as a product of Trusting Yourself.

The perspective from which the Tules arise is based in a framework of Ethics, specifically as distinguished from Morality. In this conception Ethics may be seen as founded in a respect for those rules of rightness derived through the long experience and works of humanity. Alternatively, Morality is seen as limited to relying only upon those rules of rightness founded in the gifts of guidance supplied by your individual conception of the Infinite Divine (or the unspeakable, unknowable, unmentionable for some).

The reason for this view is the belief that strength in relationships is most affirmed by that consistency in human affairs rising from common experience rather than the isolation of individual perception.

We live here as the hands, hearts and minds of all the impressions of the Divine (     ) both able and willing to allow our continued existence. If there is some single Divine Being (     ), does it not stand as logically correct that such a Being (     ) would be enthusiastic to see our bringing into daily-life existence all the best we can by using our received faculties to their fullest? Would such a One (     ) not encourage us and find joy in seeing our enthusiastic Willingness to Trust ourselves?

Is it possible that Trusting in ourselves and collectively in each other is a primary component of our given human task? Can it be that Trusting Yourself may also make it easier to trust others, and lead to healthy relationships and a wider field for happiness in general?

In addressing all the questions you may have found or may ever find in this book, when you lack any guidance stay aware that while the field of life is relationship, it can also be said that you are ultimately alone in being, even though all your choices still nonetheless have an impact in the totality of consciousness that is us all.

Please then always look to choosing in the manner that respects an ethically good solution. That you will do so is the final intent of this book. How you can begin making that easier will be seen in the next section.

## Love Yourself

The symbol is a heart, containing again the face of the Self.

Loving Yourself includes giving to yourself every fiber of kindness you have ever known or dreamed could be. All of compassion. All of friendliness. All of the caring that allows you to recognize your own needs. Absolute self acceptance, tolerance, and forgiveness. All you are that serves your personal ability to survive in any level of happiness and the expansion of Love. All the best of everything you have ever thought, dreamed, or imagined about how a happy, mature kindness would share itself with others, granted first to yourself. This is motionless activity about which you need not ever speak to anyone.

You are giving life to all that supports the genuineness of being, residing at the heart of who you are. Loving Yourself occurs prior to stepping forth into relationship with any other persons or circumstances at all. This Tule depicts the foundation of the nature of your personal ground of being, even of your very existence.

Loving Yourself also includes politely releasing support for all that does not fulfill the very best of who you are, consistently averting both self-destruction and harm that might be done to others.

Accepting the reality of this state of consciousness does not mean that you prove truth but does reaffirm the reminder to see yourself as standing whole.

From the perspective of the Earth's birth, Loving the Self resulted in the existence of the atmosphere that sustains all of the life on and around our Earth's surface. And although the Earth's continuing act of Loving the Self can be called the source of humanity's ability to survive on the planet (and so, may be seen as the foundation and source of the Lifeboat), it is not the source of human existence on the planet (The source of human existence is to be found at the meeting point between the second and third Vibrations).

Inside this perhaps incomprehensibly broad contextual viewpoint from which the Tules resulted, it can be seen as wise for those responsible for the setting of policy in human affairs to remain aware of the importance of this distinction.

If you can accept the idea that the Earth

itself has a consciousness and intelligence of its own, and if you can accept the perspective on that consciousness and its origin presented by these Tules, then it becomes meaningful to recognize and understand that sustaining human life is not an act of Loving the Self for the Earth, but rather an act of Trusting the Self. The Earth doesn't need us.

At the individual human perspective level, remember first that Loving Yourself is the single act that most sustains your existence and sources your happiness.

The personal private awareness of conscious strength is an aspect of Loving Yourself. Be kind. Life never has to end.

> *Reality is a function of your conclusions.*

7

# The Cutouts

The Cutouts following this are here so that you may immediately have the simplest kind of physical object representation intended by the author for retrieving the ideas described in this book. They are the means by which you are encouraged to allow your attention on the Tules to be more connected to the symbols and your evolving experience of them than the starting place instructions that this text is.

In making your own set, remember that the Tules are intended to be audible to your hands. The Cutouts are merely a starting place in this regard.

The Cutouts are a beginning mechanism for the suggestion that the sight of one particular symbol can hold a connection for you to far more. Much like the way the "Stop" sign can come to mean much more than merely the instruction to stop your car.

If you find yourself moved to do it, you might consider making your own set of Tules by cutting a branch off a tree and using a soldering iron, wood burning tool, or any kind of pen, marker, or paint for copying the symbols onto slices of that branch for yourself. Use a hand saw to do the cutting, being careful of your hands. Cut the slices any thickness you like and make certain that the symbols, as you finally create them for yourself are fully intelligible to you.

Imagine.

However you may choose to give life to the Tules for yourself, it remains imperative to all responsible and competent use of the Tules that you complete the reading of this entire book.

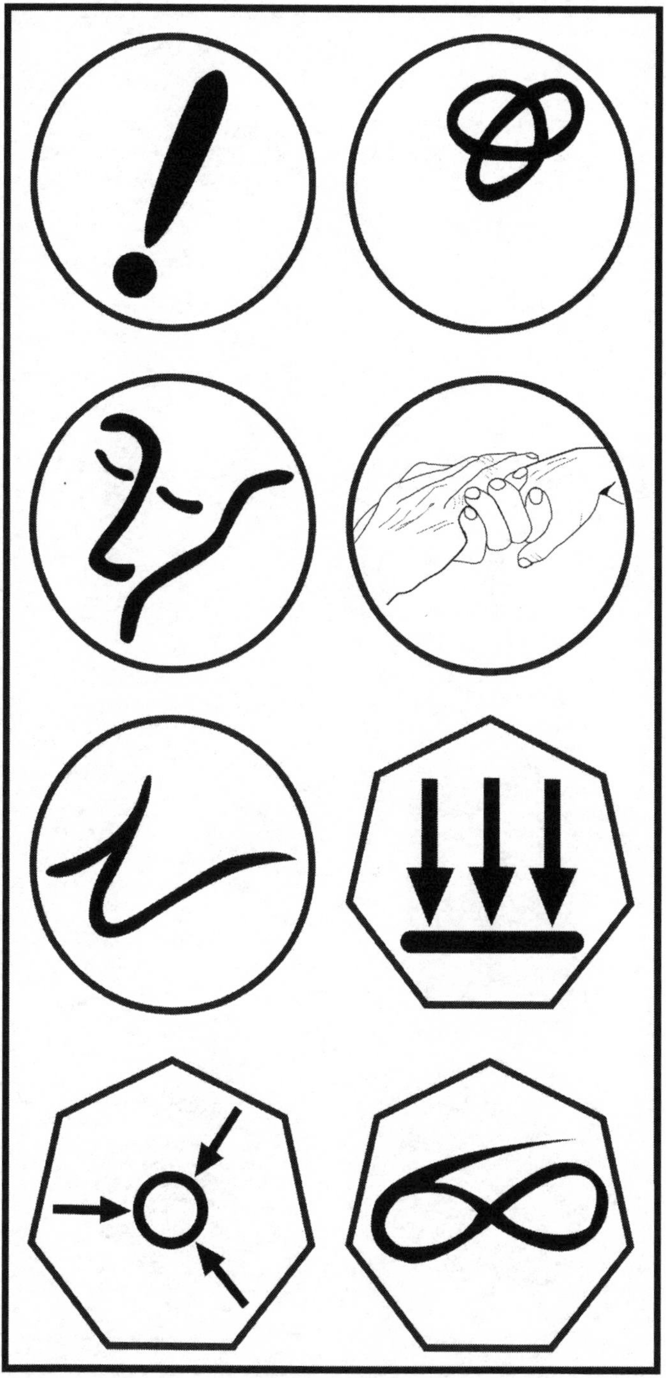

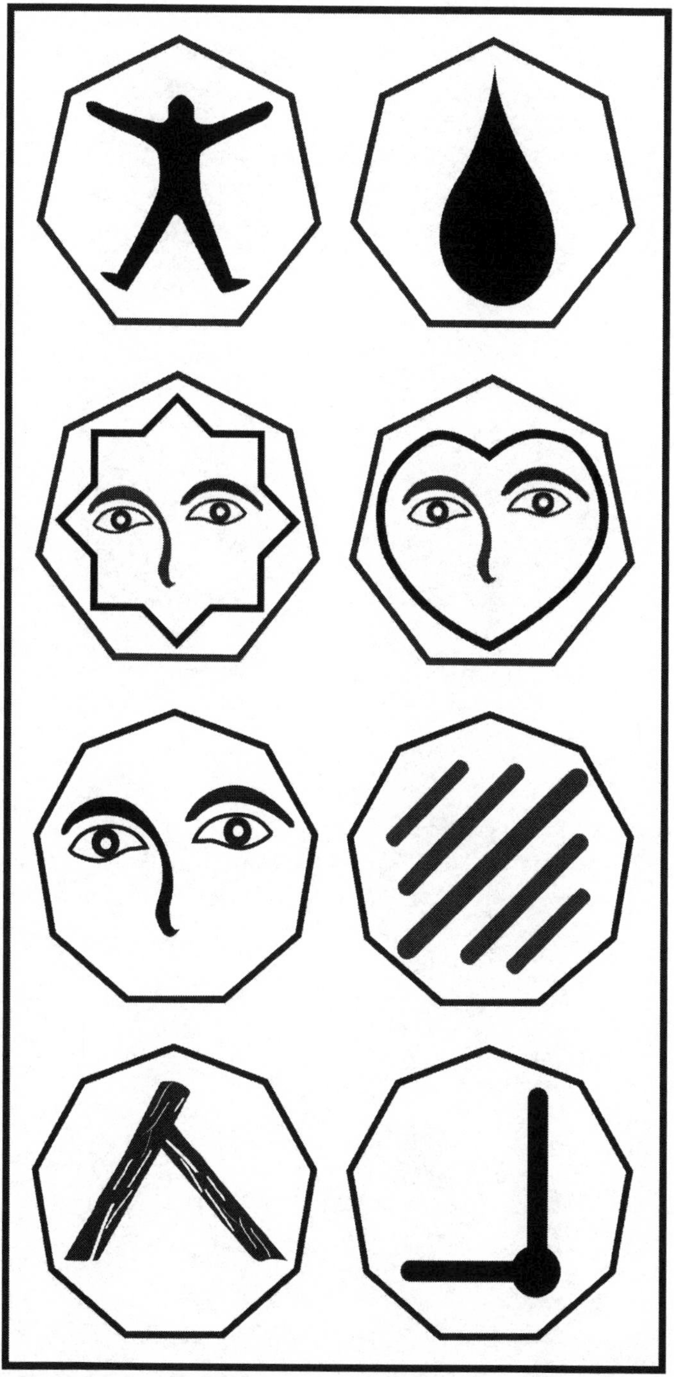

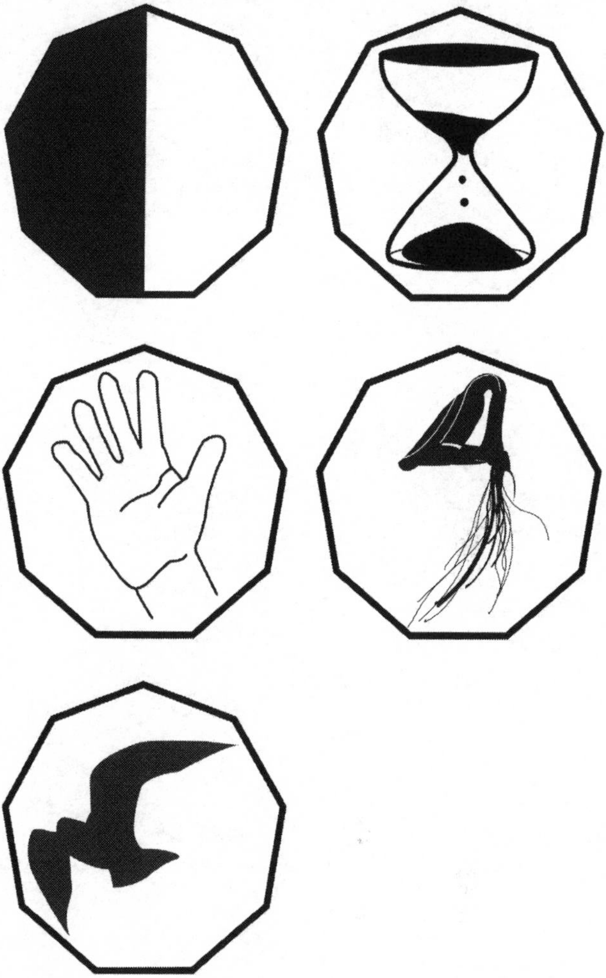

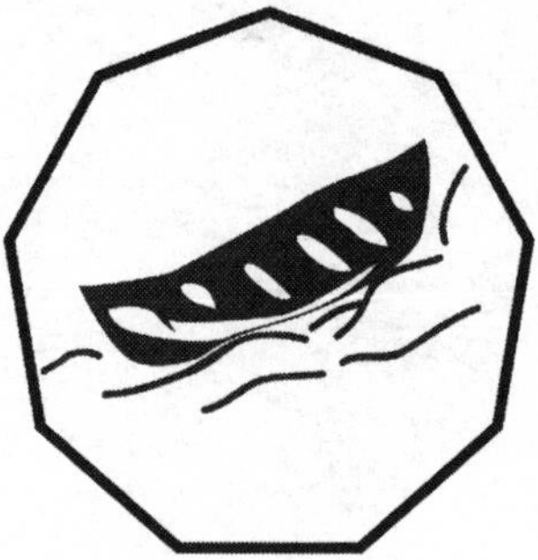

8

# End Words

There are many ways of looking at and using these Tules. Allow yourself to use them in every way you can see that your personal sense of caring for yourself, living relationship, and respecting the Earth will allow. They are intended to be an opening doorway out beyond the normal dimensional ways of thinking that we are all familiar with.

They offer infinity unraveling itself as an aspect of purpose through the thinking human mind and feeling human heart, unfolding what it holds within for you, and through you for us all.

As one specific example, consider the possibility that the Tules are offering you an invitation to re-contextualize your emotional states. They welcome you to look upon all your experience from a ground of being of fullness and a sense that all is well. You can let all your feelings be, but know them now through a new kind of doorway to personal understanding opened by the concept of Full Presence.

The room behind the door each Tule opens has the distinct quality defined by the name on that Tule, but each of those rooms is boundless, opening out upon full permission to you as the hands and heart of Creation itself.

In Love All Ways

*Tulcidious, A Vocabulary for Conscious Human Thought*


ISBN-13: 978-1511600187
ISBN-10: 1511600187

The content of this book is informational and intended particularly to be accessible for use by the visually impaired. The author makes no representations of professional authority with regard to the perspective described in this text, and accepts no personal responsibility for your use of the information this book contains.

Tulcidious is visible as a book today thanks to the enthusiastic determination of Michael Beloved and Scott Mastrow. The artwork was accomplished in part with creative and digital support from Ellen Witherite and Fumio Sawa. Ingrid Wood, Dorothy Rankin, and Joni Steiner, all presented questions and comments that resulted in meaningful levels of additional clarity and substantive explanation. The author's photo at Earth Mountain is the work of R. Erik Weigand. The further essential personal acknowledgments remain innumerable.

The meanings of most words, as presented here, are founded upon those supplied by standard English dictionaries, particularly for example, Webster's Third New International Dictionary. The word, *Tulcidious,* is of the author's invention and intended to celebrate the miracles of poetry.

Contact: Tulcidious, PO Box 600, Trinidad CO 81082
or Tulcidious@outlook.com

For additional copies visit CreateSpace.com/5417280

42847672R00093

Made in the USA
Charleston, SC
07 June 2015